THE TWO GERMANIES, 1945–1990

Studies in European History

General Editor: Richard Overy
Editorial Consultants: John Breuilly
Roy Porter

PUBLISHED TITLES

FORTHCOMING

THE TWO GERMANIES, 1945–1990

Problems of Interpretation

MARY FULBROOK

Reader in German History
University College, London

MACMILLAN

First published 1992 by
MACMILLAN EDUCATION LTD
Houndmills, Basingstoke, Hampshire RG21 2XS
and London
Companies and representatives
throughout the world

Copy-edited and typeset by Cairns Craig Editorial, Edinburgh

ISBN 0-333-54341-6

A catalogue record for this book is available
from the British Library

Printed in Hong Kong

Series Standing Order

If you would like to receive future titles in this series as they are
published, you can make use of our standing order facility. To place a
standing order please contact your bookseller or, in case of difficulty,
write to us at the address below with your name and address and the
name of the series. Please state with which title you wish to begin your
standing order. (If you live outside the United Kingdom we may not
have the rights in your area, in which case we will forward your order
to the publisher concerned.)

Customer Services Department, Macmillan Distribution Ltd.
Houndmills, Basingstoke, Hampshire, RG21 2XS, England.

Contents

1 Introduction

Following the defeat of Hitler's Third Reich and the division of Germany, the French had a saying that 'we like Germany so much, we are delighted that there are now two of her'. For centuries, Germany – the 'land in the middle of Europe' – had plagued her neighbours in West and East, with contested and shifting boundaries testifying to Germany's uneasy role in Europe. Moreover, Germany had been plagued with domestic instability too, which spilled over into bad relations with her neighbours: the social conflicts in the rapidly industrialising Wilhelmine Empire had played a role in the origins of the First World War; and the continuing socioeconomic crises and political strife of the Weimar Republic led into the brutal dictatorship of Adolf Hitler and the unleashing of the Second World War. In these circumstances, it is scarcely surprising that the French saw a solution to the apparently perpetually recurrent German problem in draconian division.

For nearly half a century, the division of Germany – and of Europe – did indeed appear to ensure a certain stability in the frozen conflict that was the Cold War. A most unlikely scenario developed: a nation of former Nazis seemed to be being transformed into two nations, one of democrats, the other of communists – and each appeared to be a model instance of its type. Over nearly half a century, the division of Germany became more and more institutionalised and accepted, such that by the late 1980s it was generally recognised that only lip-service need be paid by West Germans to their constitution's preamble committing them to work for reunification. The extraordinary stability and longevity of these two systems – in contrast to Germany's turbulent political heritage – therefore requires serious analysis and explanation. But then there was another surprise: with startling speed, in the context of dramatic changes in Mikhail Gorbachev's USSR and elsewhere in Eastern Europe, the East German revolution of 1989 inaugurated the end of division and the hurtling towards the uneasy unification, on 3 October 1990, of two Germanies that had by now become very different sorts of sociopolitical entity.

This trajectory thus poses three major sets of substantive explanatory problems. First, there is the question of the emergence and crystallisation of two very different systems – and the suppression of possible historical alternatives. How was it that notions of a democratic socialist 'Third Way', perhaps even in a neutral, united Germany, were defeated in favour of a conservative western state and a hard-line Stalinist eastern state? Secondly, there is that of explaining the remarkable stability of these two systems, once established. How was it that a nation which had experienced such political and economic turmoil in the first half of the century was so apparently successful – and in such different ways – in the latter half? How were West Germans turned into good democrats? How did East Germans accommodate themselves to communist rule? Was it simply the fact of massive presence of Soviet troops in the GDR, or was there more to the relative quiescence of East Germans (in contrast to their Polish and Czech neighbours)? And how far, under such different circumstances, had culture and society in the two Germanies diverged? Was there really still one German nation? Finally, the destabilisation of communist rule in the GDR, the peaceful revolution and its transmogrification into the unexpectedly rapid unification of East and West Germany, must be explained.

There are also broader analytical and historiographical problems. Perhaps the most fundamental relate to the fact that the Federal Republic of Germany and the German Democratic Republic were founded as conscious attempts to develop new forms of state and society, radically breaking with the immediate Nazi past, and based on

2

explicit, very different political ideologies and theories of society. They were in effect tests in reality of opposing theories of how to create a 'good' society – a historical experiment virtually unparalleled in history. The Federal Republic was founded as an attempt to institutionalise a stable parliamentary democracy on Anglo-American principles combined with pre-Nazi German democratic traditions. The GDR, by contrast, was premised on, and legitimated by, the would-be 'scientific' theories of society embodied in Marxism-Leninism – as currently interpreted by those communists in power.

But this historical experiment – this test of social and political theories in reality – was in no sense 'value neutral'. The two Germanies were created by the superpowers as anatagonistic, opposing entities: they represented the front line of the Cold War, and the hostile armies of East and West faced each other on the Iron Curtain which ran down the inner frontier of this divided nation. The two Germanies bristled, not only with armaments, but also with wholly opposing world views: they painted each other in black and white terms, as friend and foe, as all Good or all Evil; attempts to develop a more differentiated or sympathetic picture of the other camp might be denigrated as a form of fifth columnism. Even the most sober, seemingly objective, comparison of the two systems would inevitably raise problems of evaluation in the light of moral-political criteria. For example, the formal political democracy and civil liberties of the Federal Republic could easily be favourably contrasted with the obvious political constraints and repression of the German Democratic Republic; but apologists for the latter might point to the real restrictions on freedom for those individuals unable to afford the 'freedom of choice' supposedly offered by 'late capitalism' in the West, while emphasising the underlying ultimately egalitarian and humanitarian goals of 'actually existing socialism' in the East. Inherent in the latter view would be a very different conception of historical dynamics and political priorities than in the former, pro-western view.

The very concepts used in political debate were also, of course, those of academic discourse. Words such as 'socialism' and 'communism' are common currency in the cut-and-thrust of contemporary politics – and are not always used with the precision of meaning necessary for scholarly debate. The collapse of neo-Stalinist communist regimes in Eastern Europe in 1989 was seized upon gleefully by many western right-wingers as an opportunity to proclaim the 'triumph of capitalism' or the 'death of socialism', without any attempt to differentiate between democratic socialist ideals on the one hand and perversions of a Marxist-Leninist dictatorship on the other. Indeed, the occasion was specifically used for politically inspired analytical confusion. The slogan of 'never again socialism' (*Nie wieder Sozialismus*) was used to great effect by the conservative CDU against both the former ruling Communist Party (SED, renamed PDS) and the newly founded and politically very different Social Democratic Party (SPD) in the GDR's first (and last) democratic election of March 1990. This tactic of political and analytical conflation was an old one – the West German SPD had already been tarred with the brush of Communism in Adenauer's conservative West Germany of the 1950s.

Although of course constraints and influences on scholarship were very different in East and West, inevitably the political animosities of the Cold War period rubbed off on scholarly analyses, and this not only for those Germans most directly affected by division. Much Anglo-American writing on the two Germanies was also to a greater or lesser degree affected by one form or another of political bias, conscious or unconscious. More pragmatically, too, the division had effects on the nature of academic analyses. Both western and even, it seems, eastern scholars were not given full access to accurate data about the political realities or the economic performance of the GDR; East Germans had to work within certain constraints with respect to what they could undertake research on, how they could present their findings – and even what was permissible as a 'finding'; and, given the backdrop of Auschwitz, debates about the nature of the present were also in many ways political and moral debates about degrees of responsibility for, and extent of 'overcoming' of, a uniquely reprehensible past.

4

Approaches to the two Germanies

Writing in 1990, there is as yet no great body of post-unification historiography of the two Germanies. The analyses of different areas considered below were themselves developing as the entities under study changed. What sorts of approach have been developed in East and West over time?

Analyses of the GDR written by East Germans may be divided into several varieties. First, there are the official histories, specifically intended as forms of legitimation of the rule of the SED [61]. As the SED's self-understandings changed, so too did the emphases in official histories. Given their political intent, such histories must be read essentially as ideological documents. This is less true of a second category, which includes serious historical works in more specialised branches, such as economic and social history, or local and regional history. Of course historians wishing to keep their jobs in respected institutions were subject to certain constraints; but the production of works in this second category was less straightforwardly intended for public propaganda purposes, and centrally informed by a search for knowledge, in the sense shared by most western academics. Sociological research was both largely policy-oriented, and directly subject to official constraints; but even here, in the Honecker years particularly there was a more evident concern for identifying real problems with a degree of accuracy, in the interests of effective policy-making (although such research was frequently, because of its critical implications, not published). (But see [163] for a published set of relatively realistic essays.) A third category is that of dissident analyses. Perhaps the most well-known is Rudolf Bahro's *The Alternative in Eastern Europe*; a very late exemplar, published in the spring of 1989, is Rolf Henrich's *Der vormundschaftliche Staat*. As the writings of earlier dissidents, such as Robert Havemann, or of exiles such as Franz Loeser, reveal, there was potential for much broader public debate on the nature of the GDR than was actually possible under the political constraints of communist rule [3, 57, 65, 95]. In effect, a

5

full and free debate of the very important issues raised in such works was never engaged in the GDR; by 1989–90, discussion of socialist alternatives came too late. Finally, literature itself was a form of social commentary in the GDR. This was true not only of the veiled social and political discussions found in works of imaginative literature. 'Protocol literature' – transcripts of tape-recorded interviews with real people – also came to produce documents of some historical significance, although what subjects were prepared to say to different interviewers at different times must be treated with due caution [see for example 38, 85].

East German official analyses of West Germany tended to be simple denunciations of capitalist imperialism, intended to foster the 'friend/foe' mentality of the Cold War. East German dissidents were understandably less concerned with the West than their own society, but it is worth pointing out that on the whole East German critiques of politics and society in the GDR were predicated, not on a simple endorsement of a western model of liberal democracy and market capitalism, but rather on a form of humanistic, non-Stalinist, Marxism against which the distortions of 'actually existing socialism' could be measured.

Western analyses (both West German and Anglo-American) of the two Germanies have been characterised by a far greater diversity of approach, given the freer conditions of debate and publication. Nevertheless, it is remarkable how even in the West the broad development of approaches correlates, not only with changes in the two entities under study, but also with changes in the political climate of study. In the 1950s, for example, the GDR was clearly a repressive regime, encapsulated in the concept of 'totalitarianism' – which also served very neatly to establish the similarity of dictatorships of left and right, Communism and Nazism, and to establish the 'democratic' credentials of post-Nazi West Germany. Both the changing nature of the GDR in the 1960s, and a more pluralistic political climate in the West, contributed to the diversification of approaches among western analysts in the 1960s. The emphasis on the supposed powers of science and technology in both western and communist states gave rise to a new focus on 'modernisation', and debates about the possible convergence of 'industrial societies', the level of economic development being seen as a more important determining factor than differences in political ideology. The age of technocrats and 'new' middle classes seemed to be dawning, in both East and West. While theories of totalitarianism for a time fell out of fashion, they were not replaced by a single, universally accepted alternative. The relative optimism of at least some of these analyses was soon overtaken by the political explosions in the West associated with the rise of the student movement and the revival of neo-Marxist approaches in the late 1960s.

As far as western analyses of West Germany were concerned, views diverged to a considerable degree. Given Germany's turbulent political past, a lot of research was devoted to analyses of the functioning of West Germany's political institutions, the evolution of the party system, and to aspects of political culture (particularly with respect to extremist tendencies). West Germans were probably subjected to more public opinion surveys than any other population in the world. Early fears began to give way to the more admiring attempts of certain political scientists to unlock the secrets of what was increasingly perceived as a 'model state'. Similarly, aspects of West German industrial relations and economic policy management came under increasing scrutiny. West German federalism, relations with the European Community, and international relations were also investigated, from both scholarly and policy-oriented points of view. [See particularly 139 for essays summarising research on a wide range of areas].

At the same time, from the late 1960s, a variety of neo-Marxist critiques of the supposedly 'neo-fascist' form of 'late capitalism' proliferated. A very small minority took the theory of 'praxis' (which holds that the true test of a social theory lies in acting to change reality) to extremes. The terrorist acts of the Red Army Faction were intended to 'reveal' – or provoke – the allegedly truly repressive nature of capitalist democracy. Most liberals and left-wingers denounced this use of violence and restricted themselves to more arcane, intellectual critiques of the perceived shortcomings of West German bourgeois democracy.

7

Furthermore, most western radicals did not consider the repressive regime in East Germany as in any way representing a model of truly humanist democratic socialism.

Although neo-Marxist approaches were very much less fashionable by the 1980s, their heritage – in terms of, for example, looking behind formal political structures to examine the real distribution of power and the role of important economic interest groups in processes of policy-formation – should not be underestimated. And on the right, Cold War approaches smacking more of the flavour of the 1950s than of the period of superpower détente were still appearing at the end of the 1980s [6]. Between these extremes, there were continuing academic debates on a range both of specific issues and of more general approaches. While some rejected model-building, others sought to elaborate 'systems-theoretical approaches', or to resurrect the concept of totalitarianism with respect to the GDR. And public debate over – indeed almost obsession with – the nature of West German national identity and political culture was accompanied by a continuing trickle of journalistic accounts of the 'other Germany' about which many West Germans knew comparatively little. In general, one might want to summarise approaches to the two Germanies by western scholars in terms of a plurality of theoretical approaches and lively (sometimes vitriolic) debates on particular issues.

Given the fact that the period under study is so very recent, virtually all approaches are themselves part of the objects under study. Following unification, useful contributions and source materials are beginning to be published [for example, 112, 130, 132]. Many studies of the two Germanies written on one side or the other both during the time of division and, given the social and political tensions consequent on unification, even subsequently, are, almost inevitably, heavily laden with a penumbra of political associations and implications. On the other hand, it must be emphasised that historical analysis is not simply political assertion: there are standards of empirical evidence against which claims and assertions may be tested. It may be that different questions and different concepts will lead to the gathering and categorisation of different kinds of data; it may also be that all the evidence required for a definitive answer to any particular question is not, for one reason or another, necessarily available. But in the chapters that follow we must consider, in respect of each area of controversy, where the balance of available evidence should lead us by way of any more general, empirically grounded, conclusion.

2 Historical Development

How can the histories of the two Germanies best be characterised? Periodisation is simply a convenient framework for the retrospective imposition of intellectual order on the flow of events and trends. Sometimes turning points are obvious: there are key dates which stand out as denoting major turning points, beginnings or ends. But historians are often concerned with identifying and explaining longer trends of continuity or more gradual processes of change. And historians working in different theoretical traditions will tend to impose rather different categories on whatever they select and define as discrete historical periods. Historical categorisation can moreover be used for political ends to attempt to create certain perceptions of reality in the minds of the public. And it is often only with the benefit of hindsight that certain developments or events stand out as important.

The period from the defeat of Hitler to the division of Germany clearly constitutes a distinct phase, although there are important debates about patterns of continuity and change across both 1945 and 1949. Moreover, historians differ as to where the key turning points here really lie: some emphasize 1948, others look further towards 1952, as key years of decision and change.

After the foundation of the two republics in 1949, patterns of periodisation may be somewhat different, depending on what angle is being considered. For some western historians, the succession of governments and political leaders forms a very standard, traditional means of periodisation. In the Federal Republic, the first period would be the conservative-dominated phase from 1949 to 1969 (with Konrad Adenauer as Chancellor from

1949 to 1963; Ludwig Erhard, former economic miracle worker, from 1963 to 1966; and the period of the 'Grand Coalition' between conservatives and Social Democrats, under the chancellorship of Kurt-Georg Kiesinger, from 1966 to 1969). The second phase would be that of the Social-Democratic/Liberal coalition from 1969 to 1982 (first under Willy Brandt, then Helmut Schmidt from 1974). The third period would be that of renewed conservative domination under Chancellor Helmut Kohl from 1982 (culminating in his election victory as chancellor of united Germany in December 1990). Similarly, a straight political history approach would subdivide the GDR into three periods: that of Walter Ulbricht's leadership from 1949 to 1971; the Honecker era, from Erich Honecker's accession to power in 1971 until the revolution of 1989; and finally, the period of collapse of communist rule, transition to democratic government, and ultimately unification with the West, in 1989–90.

Social, cultural and economic historians would however see other periodisations as important for their purposes. There has, for example, for some time been a debate about the putative rule of the Third Reich in the 'modernisation' of German society; but some historians have been emphasizing continuities in West German economy and society until the 1960s, which many perceive as a crucial decade of social and cultural change (whatever the importance of earlier changes in the political context). These discussions have by no means been resolved. [For this author's views on the 'modernisation' debate, see 48, ch. 14].

GDR historians would on the whole consider dates of political leaders less important than phases of societal development. The official illustrated history of the GDR published in 1985, for example, distinguishes the following periods: anti-fascist democratic transformation, 1945–49; building of the foundations of socialism, 1949–61; on the way to a developed socialist society, 1961–70; the further formation of the developed socialist society, 1971–84. [For the less lavish English version, see 61]. There have also been other periodisations, depending to a considerable

11

degree on what the regime wanted to emphasize, for political purposes, at different times. [See 158, pp. 113–15].

For the moment, a rough five-phase periodisation of the development of the two Germanies may be a convenient framework for introducing specific historical debates and broader interpretations of patterns of development.

(i) Occupation and division, 1945–49

The occupation period throws up a number of interesting questions, and is currently a fertile growth area as far as historical research is concerned. Why did the occupying powers pursue certain policies with respect to defeated Germany? What was the effect of different occupation policies on the economic, social and political experiences of Germans in the different zones? How far were there important continuities with previous German history across the supposed 'zero hour' (*Stunde Null*) of 1945? How far and why were certain potential opportunities for change 'missed'? Why, finally, did occupation end in the division of Germany and the formation of two very different states? In short, why were there two Germanies at all?

The last of these questions is perhaps the most fundamental. The Allies had no clear ideas during and immediately after the war as to what to do with defeated Germany. Although quite radical plans for its dismemberment and reconstitution in a number of smaller states had been mooted during the war, such a scheme had never actually been approved. The division of Germany was a more an *ad hoc*, unintended result of factors other than any initial conscious intentions of the Allies for Germany. Many would see the roots of division in the emerging practical differences between the zones, starting already in the summer of 1945. Others would relate it more closely to the open outbreak of the Cold War in 1947–48; but opinions vary as to whether primary responsibility for division is to lie with the western Allies or the Soviet Union. And, even after the formal foundation of two German states in 1949, the question of whether the

12

unity of Germany in some form might yet be salvaged remained open, certainly until Stalin's initiative in 1952, and in some senses (including the formal commitment to reunification in West Germany's 'provisional' constitution) for a considerable while thereafter.

On the part of the Americans and British, there was a dramatic transformation in policy orientation, from an early, rather draconian and punitive approach, to an emphasis on rebuilding at least the areas of Germany under their control. By the spring of 1946 it had become clear to both powers that Germany – and particularly the German economy – must be rebuilt rather than ravaged. Britain was barely able to feed her own population, let alone sustain her former enemies, the Germans; and in the USA, the perceived dangers of communism were beginning to outweigh the desire to punish former Nazis. So there was a major turnaround in policy, symbolised eventually by the input of Marshall Aid, and the defence and support of the western zones of Germany. West Germany became an ally in the fight to defend 'freedom and democracy' against the evils of 'totalitarian' communism. This was particularly so when, after the western currency reform on 20 June 1948, the Soviets sought to cut off West Berlin from all road, rail and water links with the West. During the 'Berlin blockade', which lasted from 24 June 1948 to 12 May 1949, the western allies flew in plane-load after plane-load of supplies, and, in the process, transformed West Berlin from being a symbol of Nazism and militarism into the last outpost of western democracy. Meanwhile, French desires to strip their zone and seek maximum reparations were finally brought into line with American and British policies, with the French entering into a 'trizonia' in April 1949, only shortly before the creation of the Federal Republic out of the three western zones.

Soviet policies were in some ways more consistent, in that they sought from the outset to transform their zone of occupation into something more akin to the Soviet mould. Politically, Communists were installed into key positions; economically, there were radical land reform and nationalisation measures. But in other ways, Stalin's mind seemed open: the drastic dismantling of East German industry, and shipping back to the Soviet Union of reparations, suggested that initially Stalin was more concerned to take what he could while the going was good, rather than stay and make use of the productive potential of a future satellite state.

Although historians are still divided on the question of whether American perceptions of the Soviet threat were realistic or exaggerated, analysis of the actual steps through which the division of Germany proceeded does reveal that the western powers repeatedly took initiatives to which Soviet measures came largely in response. Moreover, division came about largely out of the power-political and economic considerations of the victorious Allies, and under conditions which might have been thought less than propitious for conducting historical experiments. This must be borne in mind when we consider the actual results of the 'experiment'. Finally, in the context of this debate, it is also important to remember the role of the Germans themselves in division: for one thing, in co-operating with the respective Allies and acquiescing in the processes leading to division; and for another – not least in importance – through having first unleashed the war which had brought about total defeat and a determination on the part of the Allies to ensure that Germany could never pose such a danger again.

Politically coloured arguments have also focussed on broader interpretations of the effects of Allied policies, particularly in the western zones. Was 1945 really the 'zero hour' which many West Germans liked later to proclaim; was there really a fresh start? Analysis suggests a high degree of continuity as far as both personnel and economic structures were concerned in West Germany, although of course the political framework was radically changed. This relates to the issue of 'missed opportunities': would alternative policies really have been feasible?

Some historians have pointed rather disapproving fingers at the American and British proclivity for disbanding indigenous anti-fascist groups ('antifas'); for hindering the development of trade union and social democratic organisations while aiding those of employers and right-wingers; for blocking socialisation measures supported by some German regional governments; for turning denazification into a tangle of bureaucratic procedures, encouraging a degree of aggrieved self-justification and white-washing rather than any real confrontation with the past, and allowing the 'big fish' to escape while only the 'small fry' were netted; for failing to effect land reform, or radical reform of the education system. Others have suggested that the western Allies did a good job in difficult conditions. On this view, there was only minority support for anti-fascist groups; there would have been little benefit to be gained from nationalising a ruined economy; failing to support employers and technical experts would have only prolonged chaotic conditions which would have allowed communism to spread; unwillingness to forgive former Nazis and accept them back into society would have provided a breeding ground for discontent from the right. In support of this view – and whatever the moral rectitude of the former view – an appeal might be made to the very different conditions obtaining after German defeat in the First World War – with all the serious consequences which followed.

As far as the Soviet zone is concerned, there are comparable debates. Many important areas remain the subject of contention, particularly in connection with the imposition of a hard-line communism. Why, for example, did the SPD finally accede to a forced merger with the KPD to form the SED (Socialist Unity Party) in April 1946? Could more effective opposition have been put up in any way to increased communist control of other political and social organisations, or to the effective Stalinisation of the SED itself (as a 'party of a new type') in 1946? How did local populations actually experience and respond to the dramatic changes affecting their lives, and seek strategies for adaptation and survival under new conditions? Although important local studies are beginning to be published, a great deal more work will no doubt now be possible on both Stalin's policies, and their effects on those who lived in the Soviet zone of occupation.

What is clear is that by the time of the formal foundation of the two Republics in 1949, neither side looked like a promising candidate for future success. There was, it is true, something of an economic upturn on the West German side; but opinion polls reveal that a high proportion of West Germans were still anti-democratic in political orientation, and prone to grumble about the miseries of everyday life and the unfairness of denazification procedures. On the Soviet side, only a minority of the population were committed Communists: most were hoping that present arrangements would prove to be transitory, and in the meantime tried to make the best of things – or left for the West. Given the imposition of new political forms on such apparently unpromising soil, it is all the more surprising that the two German states in the event proved so long-lived and relatively stable.

(ii) Crystallisation, 1949–61

Many Germans in the early post-war period hoped for a new beginning in German politics: they harboured visions of a 'Third Way', a form of democratic socialism that would lie between the devil of Stalinist communism and the deep blue sea of conservative capitalism. On some views, crucial opportunities were missed when the future of Germany might have been cast very differently. Although related to the issue of whether Germany would be divided or united – many adherents of Third Way views hoped for a united, neutral, non-militarised Germany – this question is also distinct. Even given that there were to be two Germanies, neither might have turned out quite the way it did. At the beginning of the 1950s, the respective successes of Konrad Adenauer in the West and Walter Ulbricht in the East could not have been predicted with any certainty. Both had to deal, in different ways, with a range of challenges to their regimes.

16

The controversial role of Konrad Adenauer – who in 1949 was only narrowly elected Chancellor, by one vote, of a coalition government – was highly important in determining the course of subsequent West German history. A conservative Rhineland Catholic, he was prepared to jettison the (predominantly Protestant) East Germans to their fate under Soviet domination in favour of speedy integration in western economic, political and military alliances. Adenauer's orientations corresponded very closely with those of the western allies, particularly the USA, as for example in their unwillingness to treat seriously Stalin's note of March 1952 proposing an apparently genuinely intended scheme for reunification [146, pp. 409–59]. American political considerations – the 'containment' of communism – went along with economic considerations, in particular the expansion of markets in Europe (fostered by Marshall Aid). This too in numerous ways aided Adenauer's position. The rapid economic growth or 'economic miracle' of the 1950s (based not only on Marshall Aid) played a major role in anchoring public support for the new democratic regime in the western part of divided, defeated Germany and in the growth of popular support for the CDU/CSU. Nevertheless, the end of Adenauer's chancellorship was not without its problems. His resignation finally came in 1963, under rather a cloud, in the wake of the 'Spiegel affair' of autumn 1962. Following an article in the news magazine *Der Spiegel* which criticised government defence policy, *Spiegel*'s offices had been raided, journalists had been peremptorily arrested, and Adenauer and his defence Minister Franz Josef Strauss had misled the Bundestag, giving rise to serious accusations of attempting to muzzle public debate. There were also criticisms of Adenauer's willingness to incorporate former Nazis in the new, bourgeois, materialist and self-satisfied Federal Republic, while suppressing initiatives for radical reform and real breaks with a compromised past. And Adenauer's autocratic style of government gave rise to a new political concept, 'Chancellor democracy'.

In the GDR, Ulbricht faced serious challenges, both to his own leadership and to the rule of the party. Ironically,

17

he was narrowly saved from machinations in Moscow to remove him from power, following Stalin's death in spring 1953, by the eruption of the uprising of 17 June 1953. This in the event provided him with the opportunity to build on an earlier purge of party membership to effect the exclusion of many former Social Democrats from the ranks of the SED. In 1956, and again in 1958, Ulbricht successfully dealt with factionalism in the higher ranks of the SED, such that by the end of the 1950s he was in command of a well-disciplined party of committed communists. Moreover, the institutions of the state were increasingly brought under party control, as with the abolition of the *Länder* (provinces with their own regional governments) in 1952 and their replacement by smaller *Bezirke* (districts), more easily brought under central control, and with the abolition of the Upper House of Parliament, which had nominally represented the regions, in 1958. Ministries too were adapted to ensure effective communist control of all areas of policy. Radical transformations in the East German economy proved less successful. Central planning and a focus on heavy industry were both inefficient and detrimental to consumer interests, while the collectivisation of agriculture in 1952–53 and 1960 created major dislocations in the food supply and occasioned mass disaffection. Continued haemorrhaging of young, skilled labour, as thousands fled to the West in search of better prospects, led to the eventual erection of the Berlin Wall in August 1961.

On the domestic front, oppositional forces in each Germany were disadvantaged by the roles of the USA and USSR respectively, as well as lacking, for one reason or another, adequate domestic support for their programmes. Neutralist and anti-militarist sentiments in West Germany did not accord well with American plans for NATO, while the SPD's inherited Marxist rhetoric appeared a serious electoral liability – particularly in face of the actualities of communist rule in the GDR – and in the end was jettisoned in the Bad Godesberg meeting of 1959. In the East, returning exiles and others of a humanist Marxist persuasion soon found force and repression a rather serious obstacle to their hopes. Explanation of the failures of dissenting forces or proponents of a 'Third Way' – the desire for a form of democratic socialism, rather than either Stalinist dictatorship or conservative capitalism – on both sides have been various: while some castigate alleged failures of nerve or strategy, others emphasize overwhelming obstacles; yet others suggest such visions were unrealistic to start with.

As far as the international situation of the two Germanies was concerned, both superpowers effectively recognised the stalemate of the status quo by the mid-1950s. Both Germanies were accorded full sovereignty in 1955 (with certain residual allied rights) and gained their own armed forces. Both Germanies were incorporated as important partners in wider international networks: the GDR in the Warsaw Pact and Comecon, the Federal Republic in Nato and as a founder member of the European Economic Community (EEC, later EC). But the issue of reunification remained. The Federal Republic was committed by its constitution to work for reunification, and under the so-called Hallstein doctrine refused to recognise the legitimacy of the GDR (or 'the zone') or maintain diplomatic relations with countries, other than the USSR, that did recognise the GDR. The latter, for its part, maintained that it was the West which had taken all the initiative over division, and now represented the imperialist aggressor and counter-revolutionary force.

(iii) The decade of transition, c. 1961–72

In many ways, the 1960s represent a decade of transition in both Germanies. In East Germany, the building of the Berlin Wall and the ensuing effective 'house arrest' of the whole of its population paradoxically inaugurated a somewhat easier phase as far as domestic policies were concerned. On the one hand, Ulbricht could relax a little with an assured labour supply; on the other, recognising that there was no longer an easy way out, people had to make an effort to come to terms with,

19

and make the best of, the state of affairs that they had to live with.

This change in the GDR's domestic atmosphere* corresponded with some important shifts in policy. In the economic sphere, the introduction of the 'New Economic System' partially decentralised the economy and introduced certain incentives along with a higher degree of responsibility for individuals at intermediate levels. The education system was expanded, and higher value was placed on technical experts, who began to feel they had a stake in what became known as a 'career-oriented achievement society' [98]. In 1968, a new constitution – introduced with much public fanfare and pretence at popular consultation – recognised the very real changes which had occurred in the GDR, such that it was no longer constitutionally comparable to the Federal Republic. The 'leading role' of the Marxist-Leninist party, the SED, was now officially enshrined, and all formal freedoms were hedged with the precondition that they proceeded from the basis of socialism – as defined by the Party. The sense that the GDR was by now a securely established state, a likely permanent feature of the post-war international order, fed into the new initiatives from the west with regard to relations between the two Germanies.

In the Federal Republic, too, in rather different ways, the 1960s were to be a key decade of transition. The 'economic miracle', or rapid take-off of the early years, came to an end in the sense that West German economic performance began to normalise, or fall into line with that of other West European countries. There were even moments of faltering, as in the mini-recession of 1965–66 which brought Ludwig Erhard's government to an end and inaugurated the 'Grand Coalition'. Politically, the decade saw tumultuous changes. The tendency to 'collective amnesia' in the 1950s – the materialism, the concern with building for the future and ignoring the past – was subjected to vehement attack by a new, younger generation who challenged the dubious moral rectitude of many of their parents' generation. By the late 1960s, there was a political polarisation of new left against 'bourgeois materialist' right, of young against old. Finally, with the coming to power in 1969 of a Social Democratic/Liberal coalition government, there was an SPD chancellor for the first time since 1928–30. Under Willy Brandt, a new *Ostpolitik* was inaugurated which culminated in the mutual recognition of the two Germanies in 1972.

(iv) The 'established phase', c. 1972–88

Whatever the continuing pain of being part of a divided nation, and however much the East Germans felt that it was they who had to bear the brunt of the consequences of losing the war, in the 1970s and for most of the 1980s it seemed that the fragile balance of terror in central Europe had at least effectively put an end to the centuries-old 'German question'. It did not seem impossible that with the passage of time, the two Germanies would grow so far apart that in future they would seem as foreign to each other as to Austria. But, as we shall see in the following thematic chapters, explanations of this apparent stability were not always simple; and, in the case of the GDR there were also important elements of instability which would become more important in the changed circumstances of the late 1980s.

West Germany, after the peaceful change of political complexion, had demonstrated to the world the effectiveness of her democratic political institutions, and allayed fears of political instability: parliamentary government appeared sufficiently well-institutionalised and sufficiently flexible to be able to cope with a range of challenges in the 1970s. There were, for example, serious problems connected with organised terrorism (particularly in connection with the Red Army Faction); and, despite some fears about restrictions on democratic freedoms of speech and organisation and the increasing powers of the state, West German democracy survived intact. The growth of citizens' initiative movements, and the entry into national politics of a new party, the Greens, arguably even indicated the broadening nature of this democracy. In the economically troubled years following the early 1970s – with oil crises and world recession creating serious difficulties for most European economies, western as well as eastern – the economy of the Federal Republic appeared remarkably resilient. As far as the welfare state, the social institutions, and industrial relations of West Germany in the 1970s were concerned, again there appeared to be some basis for the claim to be 'Modell Deutschland'. Despite increasing labour relations problems, rising unemployment, and budgetary difficulties in the 1980s, the West German 'social market economy' continued to earn widespread admiration among other West European democracies whose economic performance was less resilient to world recession.

Similarly, Honecker's GDR seemed to be a bastion of the eastern bloc, its economy more successful than the economies of its neighbours, its communist rule less threatened by popular challenges to the regime than were the governments of neighbouring Poland or Czechoslovakia. Honecker's proclaimed 'unity of economic and social policy', his emphasis on consumer satisfaction now rather than utopia tomorrow, and his relaxation in certain spheres (initially culture, from the late 1970s religion) also seemed to point the way forwards to an at least acceptable form of social compact with the citizens of the GDR. Seen by some as 'Moscow's German ally' [21], the GDR was generally regarded as the most stable and productive state in the eastern bloc. Moreover, in the course of improved relations between the two Germanies in the 1980s – culminating in Honecker's visit to West Germany in 1987 – the GDR seemed to be carving out a certain distinctive space for itself in relation both to the USSR and the West.

But there were also in both Germanies, critical voices and tendencies towards change. With the stationing of nuclear missiles on German soil, peace campaigners in East and West became increasingly active; environmentalists raised issues of international pollution to a central agenda; and of course the international context (and particularly the interests and capacities for action of the

Soviet Union) were changing too. So the 'established phase' was by no means static.

There are a number of important questions connected with this period. How far did the two Germanies diverge into different entities, with different social and cultural patterns, and different conceptions of their national identity, as well as the obvious – and to a degree imposed – differences in political and economic structure? And how does one account for, interpret – or even explain away – the apparent success and stability of the GDR, given what we now know about the sequel: the extraordinarily rapid collapse of communist rule, and of the East German economy, in the autumn of 1989? A predominant answer to the question of East German stability was often given in terms of repression and force; a simplistic answer to its end was based on the fact of material misery. But neither of these is alone sufficient to account for the dynamics of the GDR's development and ultimate demise, as we shall see.

(v)   The end of the two Germanies, 1989–90

In the early summer of 1989, a reforming regime in Hungary began to dismantle the fortified border with Austria. Many East Germans on holiday in Hungary decided to seize the opportunity to flee west. As the stream of refugees through Hungary became a flood, other East Germans decamped to West German embassies in Prague and Warsaw, posing a major crisis and embarrassment for a regime which was just preparing to celebrate its fortieth anniversary. Attempts to close the GDR's border even with Czechoslovakia merely underlined the essential bankruptcy of any claim to legitimacy on the part of Honecker's government. Meanwhile, domestic forces began to exert pressures from within the GDR on the ageing leadership. While dissidents helped to found the New Forum and other new political pressure groups, and organised mass demonstrations in favour of change, so at the same time reforming voices in the ruling SED itself, who had been frustrated by Honecker's resistance to Gorbachev's ideas, began to consider the possibility of introducing certain reforms from above.

In the event, replacing Honecker by Egon Krenz on 18 October 1989 and announcing a limited series of reforms failed either to stem the flow of refugees or to quell the rising tide of protests on the streets. The final concession – the announcement on 9 November 1989 of unrestricted travel to the West – precipitated a major turning-point. With the breaching of the Berlin Wall, the floodgates were opened. In the following weeks and months, it became increasingly clear – even to the reformers who had wanted to democratise a still independent, socialist GDR – that, once open to the lures and competition of the West, the GDR was no longer viable. With surprising speed, the SED renounced its claim to a monopoly on power. Following a short period under the 'round-table' government under the leadership of the moderate Communist Hans Modrow, elections were held on 18 March 1990. The decisive vote in favour of conservative parties supported by the western ruling CDU revealed a general desire for unification with the West as fast as possible.

This unification was perhaps effected a little too fast, as it later turned out. Currency union on 1 July 1990 merely precipitated the collapse of the East German economy, with snow-balling unemployment figures exacerbating the personal strains and uncertainties of East Germans in a world in turmoil. After the completion of complex international negotiations in the 'two-plus-four' talks (the two Germanies and the four victorious powers from the Second World War) and ratification by the states involved in the Conference on Security and Co-operation in Europe (CSCE), unification of the two Germanies was formally celebrated at midnight on the night of 2/3 October 1990. With startling speed – within less than a year of the hollow fortieth birthday celebrations presided over by Erich Honecker, under the somewhat critical eye of his distinguished visitor, Mikhail Gorbachev – the GDR had

24

ceased to exist, becoming absorbed as a series of newly reconstituted *Länder* in an enlarged Federal Republic. Few would have predicted, at the beginning of 1989, that a whole historical era would so soon be over. [For a more extended narrative, see 48, ch. 13].

There are a number of elements to be considered in the ultimate collapse of the GDR and the unification of Germany. These include, first, the role of different groups among the East German people themselves in making the revolution: the role of domestic dissent in the GDR, pressurising for reforms of the neo-Stalinist dictatorship of Honecker's later years, as well as the role of mass disaffection and desire to abandon the GDR, which was given its opportunity with the opening of Hungary's borders to Austria in the summer of 1989. But equally important are factors concerning the international situation, and particularly the policies towards eastern Europe generally and the GDR in particular, of the Soviet Union under the leadership of Mikhail Gorbachev, whose role in both permitting and even to some degree powering the East German revolution was crucial to its success. There is, too, the issue of the ways in which East German elites responded to the regime crisis occasioned by changes in the international context and the challenges from below in the late summer and autumn of 1989. A further, and rather separate, set of questions is thrown up by the rapid unification of the two Germanies in 1990. Clearly the various responses of politicians to the problems and opportunities caused by the falling of the Wall are crucial here. So too are the economic and social consequences of the collapse of East Germany and its effective takeover by the West.

Each of these phases of development throws up its own particular problems, both in respect of detailed factual knowledge and of wider interpretation. One way of cutting into the problems is to consider different areas thematically. In the following three chapters, particular areas are placed under scrutiny – politics, economy and society, patterns of culture – particularly with respect to the periods

25

of crystallisation, transition, and the established phase. Chapter 6 then turns to the collapse of the GDR and the unification of the two Germanies in more detail. We can finally return, in Chapter 7, to more general considerations and reflections on the histories of the two Germanies.

3 Politics

The clearest contrast between the two Germanies is that between their respective political systems. It is here too that debates between different theoretical positions have perhaps the starkest political overtones. Characterisation has often involved a high degree of evaluation. For some analysts, there was a temptation to seek an all-encompassing concept (democracy, dictatorship) which was deemed, by labelling the whole of a system, to explain all its features. Others, however, have felt that such attempts served to obscure more than explain.

The western rhetoric of the Cold War focussed on the issue of 'freedom and democracy' against 'totalitarian dictatorship'. Western liberal notions of human rights – rights to freedom of speech, freedom of association, freedom of travel – were counterposed to the repression of civil liberties under communism. But such stark Cold War contrasts never quite captured the complexities of reality, whatever the considerable grains of truth they contained. The rejection of the GDR as a 'totalitarian' state, more or less equivalent to Stalin's Russia and Hitler's Germany – the prevalent view of westerners in the 1950s – also came to be modified in the light both of changes within the GDR and changing models of political systems. Although some westerners still clung to the notion of totalitarianism, others sought new ways of characterising the functioning of the East German political system in a more differentiated fashion. Even more was this the case for those East German critics of the GDR who had a very real, practical interest in understanding the balance of forces within a system which they were committed to trying to change from within.

Moreover, West German democracy also posed certain questions. For one thing, there was an important set of questions concerning why Bonn democracy had been so much more successful than Weimar democracy. What factors were most important in explaining its longevity: what, for example, was the role of constitutional provisions as compared with economic success, or changes in political culture, and, if the latter, how had crucial changes come about? For another, what actually were the limits and real character of the particular version of 'democracy' operating in the Federal Republic? Critics were able to point to many shortcomings: to the restrictions on participatory (as opposed to representative) 'democracy', given the concentrations of power with political parties and a range of economic organisations, associations and unions, in a system of 'corporatism'; to the increasing powers of the state; to the very real limits on individual 'freedom' posed by social inequality, poverty, or ethnic minority status. The revival of neo-Marxist theories in late-1960s West Germany spawned a variety of 'critiques' of the 'repressive tolerance' of West German democracy, which was not always seen as the 'model state' some less radical political scientists held it to be.

In pursuing these issues, it will be helpful first to outline the formal political systems of the two Germanies.

(i) Political systems

The constitutions of the two Germanies, when they were created in 1949, were formally rather similar. Both were federal states, with lower and upper houses of parliament, and ceremonial Presidents in addition to the political leader (Chancellor in the West, Prime Minister in the East). But even in 1949, the systems were very different in practice. Free competition among a range of political parties in the West contrasted markedly with the built-in domination of the SED, which effectively controlled the small puppet parties and mass organisations, in the East. The GDR was based on a rather different understanding of 'democracy' than that current in the West. On the Marxist-Leninist view, the Communist party had a leading role to play in guiding society through a period of transition, when the old order had not yet been fully disposed of and the masses might still be suffering from the 'false consciousness' bred in them by capitalist society and its ideologies. The 'dictatorship of the proletariat' would have to be spearheaded by the vanguard party, with no respect for free competition among competing views. The early politics of a common 'anti-fascist front' (somewhat shallow even in the early occupation period, as the forced merger between SPD and KPD in April 1946 revealed) gave way, from 1948, to a more forceful imposition of communist rule. Nevertheless, the block parties (NDPD, LDPD, DBD, CDU) and mass organisations – notably the Confederation of Free German Trade Unions (FDGB), the Free German Youth (FDJ), the Democratic Association of German Women (DFD), and the League of Culture (KB) – also had important roles to play, in acting as 'transmission belts', upwards as well as downwards, to different sectors of society.

As the Communists increased their control, excluding former Social Democrats from the SED and establishing party control over the state, so the formal constitutional structure in the GDR was also altered to correspond increasingly to reality. The regions, or *Länder*, were abolished in 1952, and the upper house of parliament followed the regions into oblivion in 1958. The role of President was replaced by a collective head of state, the Council of State, on the death of Wilhelm Pieck in 1960. A new constitution in 1968 enshrined, formally, the leading role of the Marxist-Leninist party; an amended constitution in 1974 stressed the relationship with the USSR, and emphasised the distinctive identity of the GDR as a separate nation state. There was formally a dual set of hierarchies, but in practice the hierarchy of state (with its formal head the Council of State, its government the Council of Ministers, its national parliament the Volkskammer, and regional and local representative bodies) was shadowed and dominated by the parallel hierarchy of the SED. This was similarly organised on the principle of democratic centralism, with

29

a hierarchy of power and authority running down from the First Secretary and Politburo at the top, through the Central Committee, the national party conferences and congresses, the regional and local party organisations, right down to the level of 'basic organisations', workplace and residentially-based cells.

The 1949 Basic Law of the Federal Republic was designed with an acute regard for the failure of Germany's previous attempt at democracy in the Weimar Republic. Intended safeguards against a repeat performance included: a combination of proportional representation with 'first-past-the-post' directly elected constituency MPs; a 5 per cent hurdle, such that small parties which failed to gain 5 per cent of the national vote (or a directly elected MP) would not gain national representation and create difficulties of viable coalition formation; a more purely ceremonial role for the President, who was to be elected by an electoral college rather than mass popular vote; and a device, known as the 'constructive vote of no confidence', intended to ensure that Chancellors could not be ousted without a nominated successor who could command parliamentary support, failing which a national election would be held. Political parties were to con-tribute to forming the political will of the people, and there were detailed regulations concerning their funding, organisation and activities. Parties which did not uphold the 'free-democratic' basic tenets of the constitution could be banned, as were the right-wing Socialist Reich Party (SRP) in 1952, and the Communist Party of Germany (KPD) in 1956. (The latter was permitted a resurrection as the DKP in 1968). A constitutional court in Karlsruhe had power to adjudicate on constitutional issues.

One particular feature of the Federal Republic – as of course its name implies – is the federal system. Germany had a long history of regional particularism, dating from its origins in the decentralised mediaeval Holy Roman Empire (which came to an end in 1806), and preserved through the Confederation of 1815–66, the unified Imperial Germany of 1871–1918 and the succeeding Weimar Republic which ended with Hitler's accession to power in 1933. Hitler of course sought to abolish the autonomy of the regions. But even in Imperial and Weimar Germany, the federal system was somewhat out of balance due to the dominance of one state: Prussia. With the effective partition and dismemberment of this state in 1945, followed by its formal abolition in 1947, the federalism of the Federal Republic of Germany differed somewhat from its pre-Nazi predecessors. States such as Bavaria (expanded from its mediaeval core in 'old Bavaria' by Napoleon, and inventing a host of 'traditions' in the nineteenth century), or the proud, formerly independent Hanse town of Hamburg, had long histories and well-defined profiles. Others were however either more recent amalgamations (Baden-Württemberg) or, as in the case of North-Rhine Westphalia, a quite new creation. West Berlin retained a distinctive status as a part of a city formally still under four-power control, but in practice, so far as possible, incorporated as a functioning part of the federal system. The constituent states of the Federal Republic remained important centres of regional government, and had a powerful input into national political processes through the upper house of parliament, the Bundesrat. They also, from the 1970s, began to develop new modes of co-operation and equalisation of conditions among themselves. The federal system of West Germany appeared to have resolved the problem of harmonising a relatively high degree of regional particularism in a traditionally decentralised country with the demands on central government in an advanced industrial state. The decentralisation of the Federal Republic was to some extent underlined by the loss of the former capital, Berlin. The 'provisional' capital of the new rump state, Bonn, was modest and unpretentious – merely a 'small town in Germany' – and governmental functions were physically separated from the financial centre of Frankfurt or the multiplicity of cultural centres across the country.

The Basic Law was sufficiently flexible to develop, along with the development of the Federal Republic, without a fundamentally new constitution being required. Critics have suggested that certain amendments (such as the emergency legislation of the 1960s) fundamentally altered the balance of the constitution and rendered it less democratic. Others

31

have praised the Basic Law as providing the foundation for the stability of West German democracy – and the flexibility to incorporate the newly reconstituted *Länder* of East Germany as a means to unification in 1990. Certainly the Basic Law provided a framework for a more successful and democratic state than in the past, although the success of West German democracy in practice has a lot to do with factors other than formal constitutional provisions. Not least in importance is economic success, to which we shall turn in Chapter 4. But other changes, too, including the sheer passage of time, the passing of generations, and the incorporation in new structures and processes, increasingly made West Germany appear less like the rump of a severed nation, the threatening remnants of a defeated Nazi past, and increasingly like a 'normal' western democracy, an acceptable variant of typical political patterns, and one which many western observers felt was worth analysing and in some respects even emulating.

To understand fully the political dynamics of the two Germanies, it is inadequate to remain at the level of formal analysis of systems. We must consider the development and actual functioning of political life over time.

(ii) Political developments in West Germany

There were major changes, first of all, in the parties which represented important pillars of West German democracy. In the early years – from the foundation or refoundation of parties in the occupation period to the early 1950s – the party system looked rather similar to that of the Weimar Republic: there was a multiplicity of parties, some representing very specific groups (such as the refugees and expellees), while others were more broadly based. It was not at all clear that problems of stable coalition formation – despite the 5 per cent rule – would not plague Bonn democracy in the manner of the Weimar Republic.

But in the course of the 1950s, two major changes took place. First, the CDU – in the light of the economic miracle, as well as the effective pardon granted to former Nazis who were not guilty of war crimes – succeeded in absorbing the small right-wing parties, and became a relatively broad-based conservative 'people's party' (*Volkspartei*) including both Catholics and, to a lesser extent, Protestants. Secondly in the light of the CDU's success, there was a dramatic transformation in the character of the SPD. At the 1959 Bad Godesberg conference, Social Democrats decided to renounce their Marxist rhetoric and adopt a more moderate image, seeking to become a similar form of catch-all party with broad appeal. The party system developed into a choice between two major parties, both committed to the social market economy and the continuance of capitalism, with the small liberal party, the FDP, holding the balance of power. Given the convergence between the CDU and SPD – although there still remained major differences, particularly over foreign policy – some analysts characterised West German democracy by the early 1960s in terms of a 'vanishing opposition' [77]. Under the Grand Coalition of 1966–69 between the SPD and the CDU, parliamentary opposition was to disappear almost entirely.

This 'vanishing' of parliamentary opposition was somewhat impermanent: very major, bitterly fought out, differences between the SPD and CDU emerged over the issue of relations with East Germany (*Ostpolitik*). But the period of convergence provoked, or at least coincided with, changes at the margins of establishment politics. On the left, the students' movement fed into the formation of an 'extra-parliamentary opposition' (*Ausser-parlamentarische Opposition*, or APO) and into the explosion of radical ideas and activities in 1968. On the right, the minor economic recession of the mid-1960s provided support for the neo-Nazi NPD, which had certain successes in *Land* elections in the late 1960s. Neither of these movements as such was long-lived: the NPD soon faded, having failed to make an impact at the national level, while the students' movement splintered and diversified into a range of groups and orientations in the 1970s. Nevertheless, the development of more extremist politics was of longer-term significance. Left-wing initiatives contributed to the rise of a range of social movements, pressure groups or 'citizens' initiative

33

groups' in the course of the 1970s, as well as the formation of 'Alternative List' parties. The most significant new party to emerge from these developments was the Greens. Their concern with environmental issues, and potential threat particularly to the voting base of the SPD, ensured that certain topics had to rise higher on the explicit agenda of the major parties.

By the later 1980s, the party system of the Federal Republic appeared to be in a state of flux again. The results of *Land* elections – particularly in Berlin and Hesse in 1989 – indicated a rising proportion of voters who were not firmly committed to any of the established parties, and who were to a degree disaffected with the whole voting system itself. Voter volatility and disaffection gave particular cause for concern in connection with relatively high votes for a new right-wing party, capitalising on resentment against foreign workers in Germany, the Republicans. These trends were, however, dramatically affected by the extraordinary changes in German political life associated with the collapse of the GDR and the unification of Germany. In the first all-German elections of December 1990, the CDU rode to victory under the 'unification Chancellor' Kohl. The Social Democrats, whose rather more realistic warnings about the economic consequences of unification did not appear to be accompanied by sufficient political enthusiasm for the project, lost votes, while the environmentalist concerns of the Greens were largely incorporated as part of mainstream conservative policies.

On one view, West German democracy developed from being largely representative – intended by the Allies, who did not fully trust the judgements of the German people in view of their recent history – to being more participatory. The high electoral turnouts of the 1950s and early 1960s were interpreted by some American political scientists as evidence of a 'subject', rather than 'citizen' mentality: doing one's duty to the authoritarian state. But the high turnout in the 1972 election was clearly evidence of wide public interest in the issue of *Ostpolitik* (and support for Brandt's policies). And the rise of all manner of pressure groups at local and national level in the 1970s and 1980s also indicated greater desire on the part of many citizens to participate in processes of policy-formation and decision-making [27, 153; for contrasting evaluation, 6].

This may have been a salutary development from the point of view of popular political culture, even though political activists clearly remained only a small minority of the population. But it is less clear whether the locus of power in the West German state really shifted significantly. The degree to which citizen participation has influence on policy-making on different issues (ranging from defence strategies to waste disposal) is an open question, and a range of detailed studies will be needed to answer this more adequately. Moreover, there are also other relevant aspects of West German democracy to consider.

Some analysts focus heavily on the nature – in terms of class, gender, religion – of those individuals who are elected as 'representatives of the people'. Such analysis relatively easily points to under-representation of women, people from disadvantaged socioeconomic backgrounds, or ethnic minorities, in national politics. In conjunction with other powerful groups – such as the judiciary, and the civil servants who advise policy makers – it is relatively easy to identify what may be called (in the American sociologist C. Wright Mills' phrase) a set of 'power elites'. Others have argued that the social backgrounds and personal attributes of the national legislators are, for a variety of reasons, to a degree irrelevant.

For one thing, in a federal state the locus of political decision-making is more decentralised and there are a range of subsidiary bodies involved in policy processes. For another, and only partly related to this, a form of 'corporatism' developed in the Federal Republic (based in a fairly long historical tradition of interest group participation in policy formation). Major interest groups – the employers' federation, representatives of the farming lobby, trade unionists – came together to work out the details of acceptable policy compromises before any draft legislation was put to parliament for final, almost purely formal, approval. Radicals, seeing the greater resources and power of capital rather than labour in this process, criticised what was seen as a less than democratic process of policy-making behind the scenes, which in any event completely excluded certain disadvantaged groups with no powerful lobby who would act on their behalf. Other political scientists, however, praised this system as a means of ensuring that proposed policies were workable and acceptable to all parties affected. [see for example 39, 139].

Clearly West German democracy was characterised by certain restrictions in practice; and equally, it was not without its scandals and corruption, as demonstrated by the bribery and intrigues surrounding the parliamentary debates on *Ostpolitik* in the early 1970s, or the 'Flick affair' (named after the Flick conglomerate) of the 1980s, in which illicit practices in tax evasion and the 'laundering' of corporate donations to party funds were revealed. Similarly, there were good grounds for radicals to be wary of the increased powers of the state, and the restrictions on personal freedom of speech and association, involved in the 'Decree Concerning Radicals' of 1972, and the measures taken to deal with the terrorist wave of the later 1970s. And there was some basis for the charge that policy differences between the Conservative and Social Democratic parties were relatively minor, consisting more in differences of emphasis with respect to levels of taxation and welfare expenditure, for example, than in any fundamental difference of political principle. By the 1980s, both major parties sought wide appeal as moderate managers of the capitalist state, with the FDP having little difficulty in swinging its allegiance from one to the other when it suited it to do so.

But at the same time, it must not be forgotten that for all the very real restrictions in practice (arguably inevitable in advanced complex societies) on any 'pure' notion of democracy (itself a contestable concept), the democracy of the Federal Republic of Germany had proved, over four decades, to be a resilient and relatively flexible system. The federal structure appeared to have operated well, with a degree of regional autonomy allowing space for the different traditions and characters of the *Länder*, while degrees of co-operation enhanced resources for some and ensured more effective implementation of policies in other areas. While there were still worrying minority currents of political extremism, most West Germans were whole-hearted supporters of the democratic system in principle. And despite the Federal Republic's constitutionally-enshrined status as a 'provisional', temporary state, part of a divided nation, some liberals were able to argue in the later 1980s that the Federal Republic of Germany could command a certain 'patriotism of the constitution' (*Verfassungs-patriotismus*) which, at least for some West Germans, might replace the discredited and difficult heritage of German nationalism.

(iii) The GDR: totalitarianism, monocracy, polycraty . . . or what?

The main feature of the GDR, striking to every observer, whether eastern or western, was the fact that it had to rely on effective imprisonment of its population. The Iron Curtain, and the Berlin Wall, seemed to stand as visible proof of the GDR's political bankruptcy, its lack of any real legitimacy, its ultimate reliance on physical force as a means of ensuring stability. Add to the border guards the omnipresence of Soviet troops, the extensive network of military forces, the people's police, the workers' militia groups, and – last but certainly by no means least – the State Security Police, or Stasi, and it seemed quite clear that the GDR was essentially built on simple repression.

In the aftermath of the 1989 revolution, the extent of this repression became ever more clear. The role of the Stasi in particular began to be revealed in its full extent. It seemed that files had been kept on around three-quarters of the adult population of the GDR. A vast network of informers, informal collaborators, and people in official positions had kept the information service well abreast of developments among all manner of groups. Despite the lack of an open arena for public debate, the highest ranks of the Polit-buro were kept astonishingly well-informed of the mood and opinions of different sections of the populace, and the organisation, activities and programmes of dissident groups. Potential disturbances of public order, or visible signals that all was not as rosy as proclaimed in the official propaganda and slogans, were frequently aborted or dissolved by the speedy, highly professional operations of plain-clothes members of the Stasi before the incident became apparent to passers-by [see for example 112]. Additionally, the fear of being observed or reported on, the difficulty of completely trusting neighbours, colleagues at work, or even those who seemed to be close friends, created and sustained a mood of withdrawal and self-censorship for many people in the GDR. This contributed to the 'niche society', the widely remarked disassociation of self into public conformity and private authenticity [49].

Alongside this repression went the ultimate, and, from 1968, constitutionally enshrined power of the Marxist-Leninist Party, the SED. This, with its puppet parties and mass organisations, clearly dominated the state, and was the guardian and articulator of official ideology, the definer of orthodoxy, heterodoxy and heresy.

But do these undoubted features add up to a simple description – and effective dismissal – of the GDR as a 'totalitarian dictatorship'? The concept of totalitarianism had great popularity in the 1950s, and, after a period in some disgrace, reappeared again in political science writings of the late 1970s and 1980s [see for example Thielbeer in 74]. A number of serious criticisms have been levelled against it. For present purposes, perhaps the most important is that, by focussing so heavily on certain aspects of political life, it obscures or deflects attention from other important features of the system in operation. The GDR was not simply, and at all times, only sustained against the will of members of the populace by the massive threat or use of force. Although force may have been the bottom line, the reality is somewhat more complex.

First of all, there is the issue of changes in the nature of the state, and the balance between what might be called coercion and consent, over time. In the 1960s, with an assured labour supply, and a focus on scientific and technical expertise, new career opportunities were opened up in the GDR. Professional groups, as well as those who had benefitted from the social mobility fostered by Ulbricht, began to feel they had a stake in the system. It was for this period that Ludz designed the concept of 'consultative authoritarianism' [96, 98]. In the 1970s, when Honecker announced the 'unity of economic and social policy', and – at least initially – relaxed controls on cultural production, many people also felt that the GDR was a place in which one could work for change in a more positive direction. Such views were given sustenance by the outcome of *Ostpolitik*, the eased communications with the West, the GDR taking up full membership of the United Nations, the participation in the Helsinki process and the apparent promise of enhanced awareness of human rights issues. It was only in the course of the mid- and later 1980s, when developments such as the unofficial peace initiatives seemed to be snowballing out of the control of the state, that repression again became apparent on a scale commensurable with the use of force in the 1950s. To describe and denounce the GDR as 'totalitarian' misses the nuances of these important changes.

Secondly, there is the question of the ideological justification of repression. How could the essentially humanitarian ideology of Marxism, originally designed for the 'emancipation' of all human beings, be perverted to heighten repression? There were clearly particular features of the Soviet experience which served to create Stalinism, and its subsequent appropriation in the Soviet zone of defeated Germany. Furthermore, the argument of regime supporters in the GDR was that, given the hostility of the West, and their inability to survive in open competition, the only way to attempt the building of what would – in the long term – supposedly be a better society was, in the meantime, to insulate it from the snares, lures, and attacks of the West [for example, 130, pp. 30–3]. While the immediate practical effect of such views might be easily denounced, the ultimate logic of the argument must be at least considered. This is very different from the sort of ideology underpinning the Nazi dictatorship, which used to be equated with communism under the blanket heading of totalitarianism.

Thirdly, there is the issue of spaces for freedom of debate, lack of ideological commitment, the articulation of dissenting views. Ulbricht's early attempts at total ideological indoctrination were eventually relaxed (and were in any event unrealisable). Under Honecker, in some ways it was possible to live without adhering strictly to the official world view. The effective toleration of the church, the acceptance that religion would not wither away and that Christians and Marxists should 'work hand in hand' to build a better society, was an official acceptance of an – albeit very limited – ideological pluralism in the GDR. That this unleashed forces ultimately beyond the state's control was a risk which, in the more settled conditions of the 1970s, had seemed worth taking. Had it not been for the effective collapse of the Soviet empire in the later 1980s, the outcome might have been rather different.

Finally, there is the issue of the total configuration of state/society relations in the GDR, and particularly the relations between the ruling party and what might be called subordinate elites. The enhanced importance of the technical intelligentsia in the 1960s led Ludz to perceive the incipient rise of a 'counter-elite' [96]. However, party-political dogmatists regained – or sustained – their precedence over technical experts in the higher reaches of the SED in the 1970s, after Ulbricht's replacement by Honecker, and detailed research failed to determine any particular political line or influence of the technical intelligentsia as a wider set of professional groups [7; for the military, see also 66]. Their failure to mount any serious challenge to party dominance did not, however, occasion the kind of retrospective, retributive denigration that was showered on certain members of the cultural intelligentsia (particularly the writer Christa Wolf) after the 1989 revolution. The cultural intelligentsia was relatively easily dealt with by the regime: those who were too critical or politically uncomfortable were readily exiled, or persuaded to leave for the West; the others, whether pro-regime hacks or semi-critical voices, led relatively privileged lives, with frequent trips to the West and access to western currency, and effectively made compromises with the regime (including a degree of self-censorship) in order to continue their work. (See Chapter 5, below).

Such compromises were characteristic of wider sections of the populace too. The dissident co-founder of New Forum, Jens Reich, even admitted a year after the revolution that virtually all East Germans were to some degree guilty of complicity in sustaining the regime, of finding ways of living which, in aggregate, aided the party's maintenance of power for so long [124]. The fact that as many as one in five of the adult population were prepared to join the SED says something too about degrees of political conformity in the interests of personal and professional advancement [Zimmermann, in 14].

This brings us to the issue of political dissent − or lack of it. What was surprising about the regime's final collapse was the speed of capitulation of the authorities in face of mass protests. Regime stability is as much to be explained by *lack* of effective opposition as it is by the threat or use of force (in dictatorships) or the active support of the populace (in democracies). For much of the 1960s and 1970s, East German intellectual dissidents remained essentially voices crying in a wilderness. The role of a particular pattern of political culture in many quarters − retreatist, largely quiescent − needs attention in this connection. It was only in the late 1970s and 1980s that forces for reform in the GDR began to grow and develop (initially under the protective wing of the churches), to erupt as a major political force on the political scene of 1989 − and even then they remained a minority. A comprehensive history of dissent in East Germany is yet to be written [see 5, 48, 89, 166].

Not least in importance in affecting the nature and development of the GDR, was the Soviet Union. The USSR was the creator of the East German communist state, and was also a major player in the manner of its end. Along the way, it intervened in countless ways to affect the course of development, and even (both in the early years and again at the end) to decide whether the GDR should continue to exist at all. To view the GDR as a self-contained system is to ignore this central determinant of its existence. The role of the USSR at different stages – or, put the other way around, the degrees of freedom of action for GDR political leaders – needs further research. There are also a number of other, related questions now awaiting serious attention, in the wake of the collapse of the GDR. Not least of these is the way in which the SED was able to maintain its own party discipline, and to exert political control over the military [cf. 66], in contrast, for example, to the communist record in Poland, and even the USSR.

Given the implicit, and sometimes explicit, comparisons of communist and Nazi rule, it may at this point be worth raising the concepts of monocracy and polycraty, the latter particularly having come into some favour in analysing the power structure of the Third Reich. Clearly, the GDR was a system capable of self-reproduction and development, rather than being an expansionist, destructive and ultimately self-destructive system as was the Third Reich. Nevertheless, the notion of competing centres of power implied in the concept of polycraty may be of some, at least initial, heuristic value in exploring the political dynamics of the GDR. The relations between different power bases (Stasi, SED), or personal relationships (as that between Stasi-chief Erich Mielke and SED-chief Honecker) played some role in constraining freedom of political manoeuvre. The relations between state and party also clearly changed over time, and were not always simply to be equated, or conflated [115]. Neither the party leader nor the party necessarily enjoyed a simple monopoly of power, and command of the situation was a matter of perpetual assertion and reassertion. On the other hand, there was quite clearly a vast gulf between the relatively smooth organisation of politics in the GDR, and the infinitely more chaotic, multi-centred, political processes obtaining in the Third Reich. And not only was the whole East German system more streamlined; the use of terror by the Stasi was both less in scale, and more subtle in practice, than that of the Gestapo. Finally the role of the leader in the GDR – although puffed up in a typical communist leadership cult – was actually very much less important in seeking to obtain real popular support for or acquiescence in the regime, in contrast to the charismatic role of Adolf Hitler in holding together the centrifugal forces of the Third Reich.

The differences between the GDR and the Third Reich are numerous, and adequate exploration would require much more space than is available here. There are clearly both uses and difficulties with attempting to develop concepts for purposes of historical comparison. The notion of totalitarianism was perhaps more misleading than helpful, and this partly because it both attempted to refer to too many features within one concept (single leader, single party, single ideology, ultimate reliance on repression) and embodied no real developmental dynamics. A more useful approach would be to adopt concepts referring to more specific areas, not tied together in a global bundle. Particular combinations of factors and historical configurations, under different circumstances, could then be explored, allowing for both accuracy with respect to any one case and also comparisons and contrasts with other cases. Some of the more interesting narrative histories of the GDR have in fact attempted to do this [143, 158] although there has not so far been any successful attempt at systematisation and broader application of such an approach.

To do this effectively would now require further research into certain key aspects of East German politics. Particularly important subjects of further investigation include: the development and internal dynamics of the SED itself, and the *actual* structures of decision-making, which have hitherto been the subject of speculation with little hard evidence; party relations with the Stasi (and, at a personal level, the alleged hold of Mielke over Honecker); the political orientations and roles of key elite groups, including both technical experts and the military, on which much of the western research is somewhat dated; the changing and often ambiguous role of the church (on which more below); and the development of dissenting views and organisations, particularly in respect of the proliferation of grass-roots dissent in the 1980s. It must be reiterated that at present there is infinitely less by way of empirical knowledge on political processes in the GDR than on West German politics. No doubt under the new research conditions of post-unification Germany, much more material will soon become available on these topics, allowing us in future to develop a more accurate and differentiated picture of the dynamics of East German politics at different times.

4 Economy and Society

There were clearly differences in 1945 between the socioeconomic profiles of the areas of Germany which were to
become the Federal Republic and the GDR respectively.
West Germany contained the major industrial area of the
Ruhr, as well as the coal-rich Saar basin (the Saar only
formally became a *Land* of the Federal Republic after a
plebiscite in 1957), and was on the whole more densely
populated than the areas of East Germany. Sparseness of
population was one reason why the Soviet zone in fact covered a relatively large land area, since zones of occupation
were to have more or less comparable population sizes (with
the exception of the French zone, carved out of the British
and American zones which had been agreed earlier). East
German natural resources were fewer, having to rely on the
inferior brown coal (lignite) for energy, for example. But on
the other hand, there were also major industrial centres in
the southern areas of what became the GDR, while West
Germany too had large areas of forest and heath land not
used for agricultural production. Moreover, what became
the GDR had on the whole suffered less bomb damage in
the war than had the western areas of Germany. So the
initial differences in economic profile and potential were
not great.

But already in 1945 major changes were instigated. With
the land reform in the Soviet zone, and subsequent policies of nationalisation and collectivisation, there was what
amounted to a revolution in socioeconomic structure. A
capitalist economy was transformed into something very
different. More problematic than the empirical description
of the changes which occurred is their interpretation of the
dynamics of development. Was the GDR an instance of

'state capitalism' rather than genuine 'communism'? Why, contrary to pure Marxist theory, was the 'workers' and peasants' state' not one in which alienation was overcome? Why was it not one in which state ownership for the people made the people feel they had a genuine stake in the system which claimed to be acting in their interests? What actually determined the pattern of development of the GDR economy and society, where were its strengths and limitations?

The development of the West German economy throws up rather different problems. It has often been remarked that the country (or at least its western half) which lost the war won the peace. Or, in another famous characterisation, despite being a 'political dwarf', post-Nazi West Germany was able to become an 'economic giant'. The 'economic miracle' of the first decade or so of the Federal Republic's history, and the subsequent powerful performance of the West German economy, has prompted many analysts to search for the secrets of German success. Did it lie in some unique German character trait (at work, as well as on the beach, earlier and for longer hours than the Britons)? Did it lie in some aspect of West German industrial relations, their renowned (or supposed) social partnership and relatively trouble-free strike record? Did it lie in the financial management of West Germany, with a fear of inflation harking back to the catastrophe of 1923, with highly restricted consumer credit and close control of the economy by an independent central bank? How important was early massive American investment through the Marshall Plan?

While the very real divergences between the economies of the two Germanies were acutely visible – and had major consequences for the rapid unification of the two once the protective Wall had fallen – there is, paradoxically, another set of questions which have to do, not with divergence, but arguable convergence of the two societies. Clearly the differences between centralised communist and market capitalist states, and their patterns of economic and social policy, are major. But some analysts claimed to discern a 'convergence' of all industrial societies, whatever their overt political differences. On this view, the problems of management of large-scale, complex industrial societies threw up comparable organisational patterns: for example, given the importance of the managerial class, it made little real difference whether ownership was in the hands of a number of largely anonymous shareholders, or of the state in the name of the people; expert technocrats and bureaucrats supposedly came to have comparable positions of influence, irrespective of the formal differences between political systems; proportions of manual and non-manual workers, or proportions of workers in industry, agriculture and the service sector, supposedly also changed at comparable rates. On this view, 'industrial society' was thus a more important determinant of socioeconomic profile than the differences between capitalist democracy and democratic centralism would initially lead one to suppose. (Needless to say, such a view was scarcely shared by Marxists, nor indeed by many western analysts after the 1960s).

(i) Economic structures and development

One striking aspect of West German economic development is a certain continuity with earlier trends. Although the western Allies wanted the Federal Republic to mark a clear break with the past, this was less the case in the economic arena than the political. In the occupation period, the Americans (and, under American pressure, the British) even intervened to prevent the passage of measures permitting socialisation of key areas of the economy in different *Länder*, protecting private ownership of the means of production against more radical approaches favoured at this time by many Germans. In reaction against the recent Nazi past, state guidance of the economy was to be eased, under the neo-liberal concept of a 'social market economy'; this meant that while there was to be as much of a free market as possible, there was still to be a role for state interference, both to ensure the conditions for rendering capitalist enterprise profitable, and to provide a social welfare safety net for those who were victims of the market. And although the Allies were concerned to achieve a deconcentration and decartelisation of German industry, even after the (belated) passage of a decartelisation law in

1957, there were sufficient loopholes for previous patterns to continue. In both structure, and to a large extent personnel, the post-war West German economy was characterised more by continuity than radical change. It was only in the course of the 1960s that the attitudes at least of a new generation of 'managers' (the word was appropriated in German) began to be Americanised [11]. Many distinctive practices in West German industrial relations, such as works' councils and co-determination, in fact had their origins in the Weimar Republic, while corporatist approaches in general stretched back to Bismarck's era.

In the Federal Republic, patterns of industrial relations and state/business links were developed which were rather different from those in other West European capitalist economies. In 1951 a measure of 'co-determination' (*Mitbestimmung*) was introduced in enterprises with over 1000 employees in the iron and steel industry, allowing representatives of the work-force a say in management decisions, including manpower planning – although management retained the chair's casting vote. The Co-determination Law (*Mitbestimmungsgesetz*) of 1976 stipulated that *all* limited companies with over 2000 employees should introduce co-determination and joint decision-making. In 1952 Works Councils for joint discussion of matters internal to an industry were established; the principle was extended in the Works Constitution Act of 1972. These measures provided the basis for the claim that German industrial relations were peculiarly harmonious, characterised by a 'social partnership'. Although West German workers were indeed less strike-prone than their British counterparts (for a variety of reasons, including rapidly rising standards of living and an unwillingness to rock the economic boat), much of the legislation was only introduced against considerable opposition on the part of the employers – who even challenged the 1976 legislation, although the Constitutional Court finally overruled their appeal in 1979 – and accompanied by some disappointment on the part of the unions [see 13].

Not all features of West German industrial relations built on earlier traditions; some represented a degree of learning from earlier mistakes. Rejecting the religious and ideological fragmentation of the trade unions in Imperial Germany and the Weimar Republic, a streamlined and simplified structure of politically neutral 'industrial unions' was adopted. This meant that there was only one union per industry, thus avoiding rivalries between competing unions, simplifying the bargaining process with employers (who could not divide and rule) and strengthening the union position in negotiations over collective agreements on wages and conditions. (This also differed, of course, from the British heritage of a multiplicity of fragmented unions politically tied to the Labour Party – which was founded, historically, as the parliamentary wing of the labour movement). The seventeen industrial unions in West Germany – of which the largest was I. G. Metall – together formed the German Trade Union Federation, the DGB. The DGB, along with the employers' Federation of German Industry, and the state, together took some responsibility for joint decision-making in what was known as a form of 'corporatism', seeking to circumvent damaging conflicts of interests by prior negotiation and compromise. This took a distinctive form during the period of 'Concerted Action', from 1967 to 1977 (terminating when the unions withdrew as a result of tensions over the employers' challenge to the extension of co-determination), but was characteristic of many decision-making processes over a much longer period, including behind-the-scenes negotiations between interest groups prior to parliamentary legislation.

There were of course changes over time in the structure and performance of the West German economy, within the broad limits of the much-vaunted 'social market' framework. The neo-liberalism of the 1950s and first half of the 1960s gave way to a neo-Keynesianism in the later 1960s, with – particularly under Social Democratic/Liberal government in the early 1970s – considerable energy devoted to attempted state steering of the economy. Under the conditions of world recession following the oil crisis of 1973, this gave way to a more reactive pattern of crisis management. Following the return to conservative government after 1982, neo-liberal economic ideas again replaced Keynesianism.

49

But with the FDP holding the balance of power as an almost permanent coalition partner, there was less radical changing of economic policies between governments in West Germany than in Britain: there was neither, on the one hand, extensive nationalisation under Social Democratic governments, nor, on the other, the passion for privatisation and extensive rejection of state support for essential public services (such as the railway network) or energy supplies (such as coal) under conservative German governments as there was in Britain under Mrs. Thatcher.

The economic structure of East Germany was of course very different. The land reform of autumn 1945 effectively abolished large estates, and with them the class of the Prussian *Junkers*; subsequent collectivisation of agriculture, in two major waves (1952 and 1960), was largely complete by the beginning of the 1960s, and put a comparable end to an independent peasantry. Collectivisation measures were at first detrimental to agricultural production, and contributed both to increased numbers of refugees and to the political difficulties of 1953 and 1961 (the June Uprising and the building of the Wall). But matters improved. Agricultural specialisation – such as fruit-farming – in large collectives, with associated benefits of scale, was developed in the 1970s and 1980s. At the same time, small-size allotments were encouraged to supplement supplies of produce and eggs. While the GDR needed to import grain for animal foodstuffs, East Germany became largely self-sufficient as far as feeding her human population was concerned (if at a rather basic level, with little choice of fresh fruits and vegetables).

Nationalisation of finance and industry in the GDR and the squeezing of an ever-diminishing private sector, led ultimately to what some commentators have called a form of 'state capitalism'. Under a system of central planning, the state determined levels and types of productive output, often with little regard for consumer interests. In the 1950s, quantity was emphasised at the expense of quality or even demand; heavy industry tended to take precedence over production of consumer durables. Dislocations in supply and the inadequacies of central plans led to many difficulties.

Although central planning has frequently been castigated, some commentators have pointed out its advantages in the early years of the GDR. [In English, see for example 127]. A certain measure of decentralisation was introduced in the relatively short-lived New Economic System of 1963–70, but in the aftermath of the Czech 'Prague Spring' this experiment was terminated for largely political, rather than economic, reasons. In the 1970s and 1980s central control of the economy was combined with (from the late 1970s) increased centralisation too at lower levels, in large combines (*Kombinate*).

As far as East German industrial relations were concerned, all workers belonged to the single trade union organisation, the League of Free German Trade Unions (FDGB), which was less a body representing workers' interests than a mouthpiece of the ruling SED. Communists had criticised capitalism for the exploitation of the working class by capitalists, or private owners of the means of production. Marx's theory of alienation suggested that when people were working (or 'selling their labour power') simply in order to earn wages, and producing goods designed not for their own sake but for the production of profit, then people were not able to realise their full human potential. They would be alienated from those who employed them, from each other, and from themselves, as well as from (Marx's rather metaphysical notion of) their truly human 'species being'. In theory, all of this should be overcome when 'the people' owned the means of production. But in the 'actually existing socialism' of the GDR – a transitional stage on the way to pure communism – it was in fact the state which controlled, in the name of the people, the means of production. And there is little evidence to suggest that people *felt* any less 'alienated' when undertaking long, boring hours of tedious and unpleasant shiftwork in a 'peoples' own factory' (*Volkseigener Betrieb*, or VEB) than they did in a West German capitalist factory where working conditions, pay, hours, and holiday entitlement were very much better. The fact that under capitalism employment might not be guaranteed, and that not all workers would earn wages

51

sufficient to afford the spectacular range of consumer goods, was only brought home to many East Germans in the course of 1990–91.

Clearly, given the different ideologies on which the two Germanies were based, there were very marked differences in their economic structures. There were also very visible differences in their patterns of economic development and performance.

West Germany early benefitted from a combination of the actual receipt of generous Marshall Aid and more generally the climate of confidence that such aid fostered. The West German economy was able to reap benefits too from the Korean War, and from the influx of skilled, mobile labour from the East in the 1950s. The rapid economic takeoff became known as the 'economic miracle'. Growth rates in the 1950s averaged around 8 per cent, with bumper years in 1951 (10.4 per cent) and 1955 (12 per cent) and only lulling somewhat in 1957 and 1958 (5.7 per cent and 3.7 per cent respectively). This period of early rapid expansion then led into a longer-term pattern of sustained performance, with slight recessions in 1966–67, 1974–75, and 1981–82. The enviable performance of the West German economy was characterised by unique relations between banks and industry, restricted consumer credit, encouragement for investment, and low inflation and unemployment rates compared to other West European economies.

West Germany's increasingly powerful economy came to play a distinctive role in processes of European integration, first in the European Coal and Steel Community (ECSC) and then, as a founder member of the EEC and signatory to the Treaty of Rome in 1957, in the broader European Community (EC) [see 16]. As a trading nation, West Germany's major trading partners were EC countries. While West Germany was a major contributor to the EC budget, and was not always a major beneficiary of EC policies (such as the Common Agricultural Policy, which was on the whole of more use to French farmers than German businessmen), there were certain political benefits to be gained from her role. In particular, a stress on European integration both emphasised West Germany's willingness to co-operate rather than appear threatening, and played some role – although one which it is difficult to define or quantify with any precision – in forging a new sense of identity for West Germans in the period after the defeat of the Third Reich. By the close of the 1980s, in any event, the West German economy and role in Europe were a focus of widespread admiration as well as analysis.

The East German economy, by contrast, had to run something of an obstacle course, and it is perhaps remarkable that its performance was not infinitely worse. Ravaged by the Soviets' early reparations policy, ripped from its natural links to the West, reorientated towards the less developed economies of the Comecon bloc, radically restructured and experiencing a whole series of dislocations and difficulties, the East German economy achieved something of its own miracle in sustaining a modest level of growth. Accurate figures are still difficult to calculate, given certain problems with East German official statistics, but the average rate of growth of the East German economy in the 1960s and 1970s was probably in the order of 3 per cent a year, with increasing economic difficulties and less creditable performance in the 1980s. For all its problems, the GDR economy attained and surpassed the performance of the Soviet economy, and, under Honecker, began to satisfy a rather basic level of consumer demand for goods such as fridges and television sets. Consumption of meat per capita was, in the 1980s, the highest in the eastern bloc. Notwithstanding the economic chaos and ecological disasters that were revealed in the course of 1990, this earlier, essentially difficult but nonetheless visible, relative level of achievement of the planned economy should not be completely forgotten. It was clearly not a performance comparable to that of West Germany; but it was a performance sustained under infinitely more difficult circumstances.

It should be noted, however, that the GDR had certain advantages in comparison with other East European economies. For one thing, no other East European economy, with the exception of western Czechoslovakia, started its post-war experience with such a high degree of initial industrialisation and technically skilled workforce. For another, East Germany was exceptionally well-placed among eastern bloc countries in respect of its unique relationship with West Germany. It enjoyed a special status under the 1957 Rome Treaty, since the Federal Republic insisted that its trade with East Germany be considered 'domestic trade', and therefore free of tariffs and taxes. The GDR thus constituted, in effect, a secret additional member of the EC. Since around one-third of East Germany's trade with western countries was with the Federal Republic (including West Berlin), the importance of this favourable status was not negligable. Moreover, through West German links East Germany could more easily overcome bottlenecks in the supply of materials than could other eastern bloc countries. There were other benefits from the unique German-German relationship too. West Germany sought political benefits from making favourable credit agreements with East Germany. In 1983 and 1984 large guaranteed bank loans from West Germany helped the East German economy weather an economic storm which severely buffeted her immediate East European neighbours. West German money helped sustain the East German infrastructure, in such matters as the upkeep of autobahns to West Berlin, or the restoration of historic buildings, while West German tourism (with compulsory currency exchanges) was a source of hard currency. Although difficult to quantify with any degree of exactitude, it is clear that a not inconsiderable part of East Germany's creditable economic performance had to do with the unique links with West Germany.

At the same time, East Germany developed a specialised status in Comecon, developing in such areas as microelectronics and computer production, as well as retaining traditional strengths in optical and chemical concerns. But the relative success (at least in East European terms) of the East German economy was predicated on its unique position: closely related to the West, but all the same protected from the competition of the West. After the fall of the Wall, the centrally planned economy of East Germany was clearly in crisis, unable to withstand the haemorrhage of labour to the West or to compete on unequal terms with technically more advanced western products. After currency union, on a one-to-one basis, with West Germany in July 1990, the difficulties and dislocations associated with an attempted reversion to capitalist conditions became all too apparent. Attempted privatisation under the *Treuhandanstalt* fell foul of numerous complications associated with disputed property rights as well as widespread economic inefficiency and need for modernisation. Unemployment began to rise rapidly, and associated social tensions became increasingly evident.

Meanwhile, in the West, there were strains imposed by mass labour migration, not only from East Germany but also from elsewhere in Eastern Europe. The economy of a united Germany, with massive imbalances between its new eastern and old western regions, was clearly going to face major problems. At the same time, moves towards the closer economic and eventually also political co-operation, if not actually union, of the European Community were underway, posing further challenges and uncertainties for an already uncertain future.

For all the differences in ideology, structure and performance of the two German economies before 1990, were the societies very different? What should one make of the argument about the alleged 'convergence' of all industrial societies, which was fashionable among Anglo-American sociologists in the more optimistic era of the early 1960s?

(ii) Aspects of social structure

In some ways, the development of the social structures of the two Germanies did evince a certain comparability, for all the very fundamental differences between the two socio-economic systems. With continuing industrialisation and technological development, both Germanies saw a decrease in the proportion of blue-collar (manual) to white-collar (non-manual) workers. Both also saw a rise in the tertiary sector of service workers, and a decline in the proportions employed in forestry and agriculture. This pattern was less marked in the East than the West: in 1983, 16.4 per cent of

55

West Germans were employed in the service sector, and only 5.9 per cent in forestry and agriculture; while only 6.9 per cent of East Germans were employed in the service sector and over 10 per cent remained in forestry and agriculture (compared to 17.9 per cent in 1950). The nature of the work that people actually did changed in somewhat comparable ways, although the East lagged some way behind the West in this respect [86, 145].

Somewhat more marked were differences in levels of urbanisation, with an expanding population in the West increasingly living in larger urban areas, while the relatively static (and sometimes declining) population of the more sparsely populated East remained to a greater extent residents of medium and small-sized communities, with less marked trends towards urbanisation. In 1950, 29 per cent of the population in both East and West Germany lived in small communities with less than 2000 inhabitants. In 1980, while 24 per cent of East Germans still lived in such small communities, only 6 per cent of West Germans did; by this time, 74 per cent of West Germans were living in communities of over 10000 (compared to 57 per cent of East Germans). And while East Germany's population had remained almost static, fluctuating around 17 million, West Germany's had risen by nearly 50 per cent to 61.7 million [48, p. 222–3].

On a Marxist view, social classes are defined by relationship to the means of production (ownership or non-ownership), combined with the more subjective feature of collective consciousness of common interests in opposition to antagonistic classes. In theory, then, where there is no private ownership of the means of production, there ought to be no 'classes' in the pure sense, although there will still be individual differences in interest and ability. But in all state-socialist societies which have existed historically, major group-based differences in privilege, power, wealth and income persisted – although in somewhat different forms than under capitalism. And these group differences were recognised, and indeed to some degree fostered, by communist regimes in power. They were however (at least officially) held to be less iniquitous, more socially useful, than the inequalities obtaining in capitalist societies.

In the East, there was a somewhat narrower spread of income distribution than in the West, with certain crucial qualifications. An ideological commitment to greater equality was tempered, from the 1960s onwards, by a recognition of the need to attract and reward people with certain qualifications. Thus high earners included top doctors, engineers and scientists, as well as Politburo members, ministers, high-ranking officers and generals, and regional industrial and political leaders. In the mid-1970s, while the average monthly income of employees in nationalised enterprises was 867 Marks, top earners received salaries ranging from 2500 up to as much as 10 000 Marks per month [32, pp. 54–6]. Pensioners were generally the worst-off. Nevertheless, with substantial subsidies for basic foodstuffs, housing and transport, and a high proportion of two-income families in the GDR, money as such was often less important than access to western currency or scarce goods. The long waiting lists for cars, for example, were greater stumbling blocks than any lack of money; similarly, the desirable high quality western goods in Intershops were available only to those with hard western currency to pay for them. Moreover, as far as privileges were concerned, the privilege to travel to the West – being one of the *Reisekader* – was for most people more important than level of income in East German marks. Political commitment, or at least conformity, were more important to acquiring privileges in the East than were income or wealth as in the West.

While living standards generally were much higher in the West, there was also greater inequality of income and wealth across a broader spectrum. Although some analysts wanted to claim that West Germany was developing into a relatively classless society, with universal affluence allegedly obscuring social differences, and regional accents denoting only area of birth, not position in a social hierarchy, nevertheless major differences in wealth and status remained. Most notably, a new, ethnically distinct, 'underclass' of 'guest workers' (*Gastarbeiter*) were predominantly employed in the most disagreeable and least well-remunerated jobs, under the worst conditions as far as such matters as employment rights, health and safety measures, or level of union protection were concerned [157]. And at the top of the hierarchy, the predominance of members of the old aristocracy (whether or not they dropped the 'von' from their surnames) was still to be observed. Social mobility continued to be largely structurally induced – that is, related to changes in the class structure as a whole, with the shrinking of the agricultural and blue-collar sectors inevitably implying a degree of inter-generational mobility – with the acquisition of educational credentials to a considerable degree serving to legitimate the inheritance of social status. But with a plurality of elites – in politics, finance, business, academia, the law, the churches, other professions – there was no single route to the top in what might be an unequal, but still relatively open, society. A professional and well-to-do background remained, of course, a distinct advantage – as did being male. Women in the West continued to have 'their' social class measured primarily in terms of father's or husband's occupation. Insofar as they took up paid employment outside the home, women tended to remain in lower-status, less well paid, often part-time or temporary employment, with minimal help by way of state nurseries or provisions for after-school child-care [62; see also 84].

The route to the top was rather different in East Germany. Under Ulbricht, there were positive measures to advance previously underprivileged children from peasant and working class backgrounds, at the expense of the middle classes. State sponsorship of social mobility began to be relaxed in the 1960s, when the emphasis was put on talent in the era of scientific-technological revolution, and by the 1970s and 1980s a certain reproduction of the class structure (inheritance of status from one generation to the next) had reappeared. However, most important in social mobility was willingness at least to conform, and preferably to be actively committed, politically. A certain tension between the importance (and alleged 'rise') of technical experts and party dogmatists was always to a degree apparent, although party discipline ensured the predominance of the latter. If, however, a bright young person was prepared to make the necessary compromises politically, then career prospects could be equally bright, irrespective of parental background.

There was also a certain, limited, degree of equality for women in East Germany, at least in the sense that half of university students, and half the labour force, were female. Generous maternity benefits and extensive child-care provisions meant that it was possible (if exhausting) for women to combine the roles of mother, housewife and paid employee – and indeed it was an individual's duty to work. On the other hand, given the persistence of an unequal division of labour on the domestic front, many women experienced their role as one of a 'double burden', labouring under two jobs and never having time to relax. Relatively high divorce rates and proportions of children born out of marriage reflected both the greater economic independence of East German women, and the strains often experienced in marriage; but high rates of marriage and re-marriage also indicated that personal relations between economically independent partners were still held in con-siderable esteem. Nevertheless, on balance the GDR was not a female paradise. Despite a very real ideological com-mitment on the part of the regime to the equality of the sexes – in addition to simple need for labour in a demo-graphically skewed population, with an early large excess of females over males – East German women had 'advanced' only a little. They remained disproportionately employed in the lower levels of any professional hierarchy, and almost completely disappeared (with individual exceptions, such as former Education Minister Margot Honecker) as far as the higher reaches of the political hierarchy in particular were concerned. And the atmosphere of political oppression, material shortages, and restricted freedom, affected men and women alike, giving the lie to any notion of real 'emancipa-tion', whether of women in particular or the 'proleteriat' in general.

The education systems of the two Germanies played a role in reproducing differences in their class structures. Education was under the control of the *Länder* in West Germany, and most retained a relatively traditional selective system [59]. The most academically gifted children would attend the *Gymnasium*, a form of grammar school at the end of which one took the *Abitur* (the rather broader equivalent of English A levels). Passing the *Abitur* gave access to university, with only a few disciplines operating a *numerus clausus* to restrict numbers entering higher education. Other children would attend the more vocationally oriented *Realschulen* or (to a decreasing extent) *Hauptschulen*. Emphasis on vocational training continued with efficient apprenticeship schemes and day-release courses, resulting in a well-trained work-force and the possibility of acquiring further qualifications. But, for all the successes of the West German education system, it was still notable that children from working class backgrounds appeared to have greater opportunities when the system of education was comprehensive rather than selective.

In East Germany, by contrast, after a series of reforms a system of comprehensive 'polytechnical' education, with emphasis on practical work experience as well as academic learning, was in operation for the vast majority of the population. A variety of routes into higher and further education were available even for those who did not go through the standard *Erweiterte Oberschule* (EOS, a form of sixth-form college) for the more academically inclined. A minority of children attended a range of elite schools from an early age – whether because they were identified as having, for example, particular talents in sport or music, or whether because they were children of the political elite. Again, whatever the educational institution, willingness at least to conform politically was the essential prerequisite of educational advancement: a university education or the chance of pursuing a chosen career was completely blocked for those who stood out as dissident, or were children of, for example, prominent and outspoken Christians.

East Germany, then, was clearly not a 'classless' society in any real sense. Even the orthodox Marxists of the GDR admitted to the existence of elites and privileges [see for example 163]. They never, however, satisfactorily resolved certain problems of conceptualisation or systematic data-gathering on, for example, the loosely defined category of the 'intelligentsia'. This mysteriously appeared and disappeared, or was subsumed under other categories, in the official statistical yearbooks, posing problems for western analysts restricted to such sources [see for example 145 (1984), p. 389, pp. 108–9; see also 32, pp. 47–53].

More problematic is the task of explaining the pattern of social differentiation – particularly if the starting point is the issue of how to reduce social inequalities, or at least enhance equality of opportunity. The GDR appears to have become entrapped in a vicious circle in a number of respects. First, there was the problem – in common with western, capitalist societies – of the restrictions on equality of opportunity posed by simple poverty and inequality from birth (or even conception) onwards. Innumerable studies have shown the lower brithweights, higher perinatal and infant mortality rates, and lower life expectancies of children in lower social classes; these disadvantages are followed and compounded by (for whatever range of reasons) lower levels of educational attainment, and correspondingly reduced chances of social mobility. In the GDR, environmental pollution seems to have exacerbated the cycle of poverty and deprivation in many areas. Secondly, the issue was overlain in state socialist societies by the extraordinary power and importance of the 'politbureaucracy'. While it is inappropriate to suggest (as some commentators did) that the GDR was characterised by a 'unitary elite' [86], in that there were a range of politically subordinate but still privileged groups, nevertheless the ultimate power of the various branches of the party, state, and security apparatus still posed an overwhelming obstacle to any attempt at achieving a society characterised by either a degree of egalitarianism or even simply equality of opportunity. The Marxist attempt at achieving a 'classless' society through the abolition of private ownership of the means of production could only hope even to begin to succeed if it went hand in hand with the related notion of the 'withering away of the state' – a tendency for which state socialist societies were hardly noted.

Beyond 'objective' facts having to do with inequalities of wealth and poverty, degrees and avenues of social mobility, living standards and life chances, there are many more 'subjective' aspects to society. It is to the issues of culture and identity in the two Germanies that we now turn.

5　Patterns of Culture

Patterns of culture are notoriously difficult to define and locate. This is true to some extent of 'high culture' (literature, the performing and visual arts), and much more so of 'popular culture' in the sense of the orientations, outlooks and creative productions of subordinate social groups (including both 'mass culture', and the problematic notion of 'political culture'). Furthermore, in asking about degrees of divergence between the two Germanies, can one even draw a clear baseline from which to start? There were clearly differences in religious allegiance, types of social organisation, forms of political attitude and behaviour, between different social groups and in different regions of Germany before 1945. It is difficult enough to characterise cultural patterns of any one group; to seek to do so for a whole state would seem sheer folly, if it were not for the fact that this is done all the time when people speak of, for example, 'national identity' or 'national character', or make sweeping contrasts between the supposed personality types of East and West Germans.

Nevertheless, even granted all necessary caution, there are certain diverging patterns which may be identified between the two Germanies. What makes this subject particularly interesting is the fact that on both sides, the victorious powers made strenuous efforts to 're-educate' the Germans, and – to a somewhat greater degree in the East than the West – to transform the German 'personality' into a new mould. Such explicit attempts did not always produce the desired effects, while observable changes often were based on quite different factors.

(i) Official attempts at the transformation of the Germans

Western attempts at denazification and democratisation were on the whole characterised by a degree of confusion and ultimate inefficiency. The Allies were never quite clear whether they were aiming at retribution or rehabilitation, and in the end it was the latter process which won – particularly as, in Adenauer's Germany, former 'small' Nazis (and even some less unimportant ones) were successfully reabsorbed into the mainstream of public life. In the Soviet zone, the focus was less on individual personality than on structural transformation. Removing the socioeconomic base which, on the Marxist view, had given rise to Nazism, was deemed more important than individual re-education. At the same time, given the associated political aim of installing Communists in high places, there was also a considerable turnover of personnel, although in the East, as in the West, the importance of technical expertise necessitated the retention of many former Nazis in certain areas. In the Cold War period, the two Germanies vied in attempting to discredit each other by revealing how many former Nazis held high positions in the new states. [See generally 43, 48, 54, 116].

In the West, apart from some rather limited early attempts to teach the Germans how to be democratic (largely on the part of the British) and how to be good managers and productivity-orientated workers (managerialist values associated with the American Marshall Plan), the Allies largely left the Germans to get on with the job of becoming good democrats themselves [20, 37, 123]. There were constitutional restrictions on *un*democratic parties, but on the whole the limits of permissable cultural production and political activity were broad. Indeed, the main constraint in the democratic capitalist West was simply material: profitability. Newspapers, for example, tended to be dominated by a few large profit-making concerns (notably, for the tabloids, the Axel Springer empire). This did not however preclude the publication of minority or radical views. Indeed, in literature, cinema and theatre, critical views gained a certain predominance, and in the performing arts 'alternative' views were often highly subsidised. In this way, a certain pluralism was even officially promoted.

In the GDR under Ulbricht, however, radical measures were adopted in the attempt to foster the development of a more uniform 'socialist personality'. The whole education system was transformed, with the abolition of private schools and the squeezing out of religious instruction already in the occupation period. In 1954, a secular state ceremony known as the *Jugendweihe* was introduced as a challenge and alternative to religious confirmation, further serving to differentiate between those who conformed to the atheist Marxist-Leninist world view and those who clung to their religious faith. Marxism-Leninism was a compulsory subject at all levels of the education system, from schools through further and higher education extending even, for example, to weekend refresher course for established members of the medical profession. Meanwhile, writers and artists were also to be enlisted in the attempt to impose a new view of the world. After the Bitterfeld conference there was to be a closer relationship between manual workers and the arts, as workers were urged to 'take up their pens' and write of their experiences, while writers were to gain experience of manual labour.

Energetic attempts to impose a new orthodoxy were relaxed somewhat in the 1960s. Under Honecker, a minimal preparedness to conform outwardly appeared to be at least acceptable, although of course full commitment to the regime based on deep inner conviction would have been preferred. But to some extent social policies based on material satisfaction took the place of attempts at ideological indoctrination. In the early 1970s, there was a certain cultural liberalisation, although this came to an end with the expulsion of the dissident guitarist and song-writer Wolf Biermann at the end of 1976. Relations between the regime and Christians improved in the course of the 1970s, culminating in an agreement between church and state in 1978. This accorded the church an officially tolerated status as the only independent social institution in the GDR outside the state-dominated system – a status

65

which proved to have unintended political consequences, as we shall see in a moment.

Yet for all the changes in course and cultural policy over time, the East German regime was fundamentally based in a desire to mould people into a certain form of personality with a particular view of the world. This ideological emphasis was given visible expression in the ubiquitous banners and slogans proclaiming, for example, the undying love and friendship of East Germans for the Soviet Union, or that the regime was doing everything 'for the wellbeing of the people' (*Alles zum Wohle des Volkes*). 'The people' were of course only too well aware of propaganda and censorship. It is unlikely that the official flags and posters had much impact on people's views; and, given the fact that most East Germans were able to watch western television, they adopted quite a cynical view of their own 'news' and current affairs programmes. The correlate of attempted indoctrination was also, of course, the systematic suppression, with greater or lesser degrees of force, of alternative, 'subversive' views. Censorship, adverse effects on career prospects, subtle pressures on family members – even the removal from their families of dissidents' children – were among the methods employed to instil fear among those who were inclined to 'think differently'. In the event, although East German culture developed in certain distinctive patterns, neither official propaganda nor suppression were entirely successful.

(ii) Patterns of culture

What were the effects of these different policies? And how far were observable, developing differences between the two Germanies the effect, not of the overt policies of the regimes, but rather of other factors, such as changing patterns of social and political experience?

As far as 'high culture' is concerned, there were clear differences related very directly to the different political circumstances in East and West. After an early, rather hesitant period in which Germans in the West had difficulty finding an authentic voice in which to speak, having to 'clear a path through the jungle' after the Nazi perversions of the language, a number of major writers began to emerge. Among those who attained international prominence for their writings, often rather critical of certain aspects of West German life, were, for example, Heinrich Böll and Günter Grass. But the West German cultural scene – in all senses – was characterised by immense diversity. The position was very different under the more constrained political conditions obtaining in the East. Despite the repeated fluctuations in cultural policy – in which periods of relative liberalisation were followed by renewed periods of repression – and despite the assorted tactics for evading or negotiating the full effects of political censorship, or having works published in the West which were not permitted in the East, at all times East German culture was very much affected by the conditions of production. Writers may perhaps be divided into three groups: those who sustained the regime more or less whole-heartedly (perhaps with specific differences on particular issues, or private reservations about others) such as Anna Seghers or Johannes Becher; those who, while to some considerable degree in sympathy with the overriding aims of the regime, were at least more obviously critical of certain aspects, or suffered from censorship and self-censorship at different times (Bertolt Brecht, Stefan Heym); and those for whom the constraints eventually became intolerable, and who left for the West (Jurek Becker, Monika Maron, and many others). Whatever else East German literature was, it could not help but be political, even when the subject matter seemed either intensely private and personal, or very far removed from the present.

Literature was for East Germans a channel for coded discussion of present conditions, in a way which was not necessary in the West. The West had the highbrow press – newspapers such as the *Frankfurter Allgemeine Zeitung*, weeklies such as *Die Zeit* or *Der Spiegel* – in which public debates over issues of major significance could be conducted in the open, and, as it were, in a 'secular' form. In the East, all newspapers and magazines were either directly organs of the

SED and the associated puppet parties, or of permitted and party-dominated social organisations. A partial exception was constituted by church publications, but even these were subjected to censorship. Even the 'unreal' world of fiction was subjected to censorship: but there were times when certain works could be published, and also ways of saying things which allowed them to slip through.

For a long time East German writers were the focus of much, often very enthusiastic, interest in the West. But the backlash came in 1990. Christa Wolf's *Was bleibt?* was a brief and at first glance seemingly innocuous work, published a decade after it was actually written, by one of East Germany's most distinguished and internationally renowned authors. But the belated publication of this auto-biographical account of a day under – rather light – Stasi surveillance unleashed a controversy out of all proportion to its ostensible object. The issue revolved on whether the cultural intelligentsia in the GDR had occupied a privileged position, able to publish in and travel to the West so long as certain compromises with the regime were made, and had by this allegedly pusillanimous stance in effect helped to sustain a repressive regime in power. Those whose careers in the East had been terminated by 'going too far', such as Wolf Biermann, were bitterly critical of those who had not had the courage 'to go far enough'. In the cacophany of voices in 1990 were heard many West German critics who had never experienced, and seemed barely to understand, the kinds of constraints and pressures under which East Germans had been writing. And it should be noted that many of the critical voices in the former GDR had been seeking new ways through to a better future, and were by no means simply pro-western in their attitudes. But there was nevertheless an important underlying point. Those writers who had stayed and worked within certain limits (including a degree of self-censorship) had not in the event mounted any effective challenge to a repressive state; and the stability of the East German regime had been aided by the ease with which it could export overly critical voices to a common language community, with automatic rights of citizenship, in the West – in a way that Czechoslovakia,

Poland or Hungary could not. The vitriolic nature of the public debate in 1990 was indicative of a level of tension and misunderstanding of complex issues that the new Germany had to confront.

The social and political role of religion and the churches in the two Germanies diverged, as a result of different political circumstances, in comparable ways. In the West, despite the powerful institutional role and voice of the churches, the salience of religion in everyday life declined for many people. In the GDR, by contrast, the Protestant churches in particular came to occupy an increasingly important role in a number of – sometimes conflicting – ways. (Catholics remained a rather retreatist, quiescent minority in the GDR). Subjected under Ulbricht to initial persecution in the 1950s, followed by a limited and rather artificial 'Christian-Marxist dialogue' in the 1960s, East German Protestants eventually came to reconsider their position. Since the 1968 constitution rendered their all-German organisation illegal (and joint meetings were in any case impracticable), East German Protestants decided in 1969 to form their own separate organisation, and to adopt a more positive attitude towards working *within* (rather than 'against' or 'alongside') socialism (in Bishop Schönherr's famous formulation of 1971). Such changes in stance, and the very real importance to the East German regime of church welfare institutions (hospitals, old peoples' homes, childcare centres) and other activities, led to a change in status for the churches under Honecker, culminating in formal recognition of the church's role as an autonomous social institution in 1978.

But, having gained the official status of a space in which free discussion could take place, many individual churches began to develop into centres of oppositional debate and breeding grounds of dissent. The balance began to shift in the 1980s. At first, church leaders, anxious to remain on good relations with political leaders, intervened to moderate and contain dissent: religious toleration thus acted as a form of pressure valve for the regime. But from the mid-1980s onwards, dissent proliferated beyond the protective (and often also constraining) bounds of the umbrella of the church. By the late 1980s, there were a wide range of – not necessarily Christian – groups focussing on issues to do with human rights, peace, the environment. There were also differences within the church between 'grass-roots' groups and adherents of the 'church from below', on the one hand, and the more cautious or conservative members of the church hierarchy who were unwilling to put their position *vis-à-vis* the state into jeopardy, on the other. These developments were obviously the focus of much discussion among East German participants in the revolutionary autumn of 1989, when the role of Christians was very prominant (particularly in the emphasis on non-violence and the symbolism of candles). The role of religion in the GDR (both at institutional and individual levels) will now need to be the subject of more serious historical attention and debate. [For useful beginnings, see: 29, 41, 48, 53, 63, 64, 129, 142; on the experience of Jews in East Germany, see 120].

(iii) National identity and political culture

What of the more ethereal, or difficult to identify, areas of national identity and political culture? The issue of national identity – and of overcoming the past – was one high on the political agenda of both states in divided, post-Nazi Germany, and was satisfactorily resolved by neither.

In the 1950s and 1960s, the official line in the GDR was that the West was responsible for division, and that it was the East Germans who were sustaining the notion of a united German nation. Moreover, with its proud anti-fascist record, it was the GDR which was the historically more 'progressive' state. With the international recognition of the GDR after the conclusion of *Ostpolitik*, the stance changed noticeably. In the 1970s, strenuous efforts were made by the East German regime to develop a sense of a separate GDR identity, based in a class theory of the nation which held that not only were there two German states (the East German still being viewed as the more progressive), there were now also two German nations. From the later 1970s, this was accompanied, in curious and interesting ways, by new views of German history which sought to reappropriate the whole of the German past, and to represent the GDR not only as the legitimate successor to radical and working class traditions but also to politically more ambiguous cultural traditions. Figures such as Luther, Frederick the Great, and Bismarck, received a more sympathetic hearing than ever before in the GDR's history. Visible signs of the German heritage – statues, churches, historic buildings, old town centres – began to be restored, actively preserved, rather than allowed to crumble through neglect.

While East German historical writing suffered from similar pressures and constraints as literary production, and some works were the predictable product of prescribed political views, others were interesting, sophisticated, and – allowing for the constraints of censorship – comparable in intellectual quality with serious western counterparts. (Despite this, after unification in 1990 there was considerable controversy over western decisions for wholesale institutional closures and mass redundancies of East German historians). The impact of East German history writing on the formation of a putative GDR national identity must remain to some extent a matter of speculation. As with other areas, most people could recognise blatant propaganda when it did not conform to everyday experience; and stress on the German heritage of the GDR might not entirely compensate for the stresses and irritations of everyday life. On the other hand, *lack* of exposure to certain information – such as, for example, the role of non-communist resistance in the Third Reich – could lead to serious deficits in understanding. With respect to the Third Reich particularly, there would need to be a new 'coming to terms with the past'. Despite often quite sensitive historical analyses of certain aspects of fascism, GDR historiography had for the most part presented at best a partial view (with serious difficulties over such matters as the Hitler-Stalin pact). And the rehabilitation and absorption of former Nazis into East German politics and society had been almost entirely covered up, in an attempt to represent the Federal Republic as the natural home of all former Nazis.

Politically biassed histories were scarcely the sole pre-rogative of the East. But under the pluralistic conditions of the West, a range of different views could be published, giving rise to often heated public discussions over conflicting interpretations of the German past. In the early 1960s, a lively debate on Germany's role in the origins of the First World War was unleashed by the historian Fritz Fischer. The Holocaust was of course an even more contentious issue. In the months preceding the 1987 General Election, a number of conservative historians followed Ernst Nolte's lead in seeking to relativise Nazi crimes. They sought to suggest both that German history was not uniquely reprehensible — the crimes perpetrated by the dictators Pol Pot and Stalin being comparable to those of Hitler — and that, in some oblique and never adequately argued way, Stalin's crimes not only preceded but also provided the impetus and occasion for those of Hitler. Given that Germany's past was not uniquely evil, it was time, they argued, to restore a little national pride among Germans. This view was energetically contested by left-liberal intellectuals such as Jürgen Habermas and Hans-Ulrich Wehler. Apart from giving right-wing extremist political groups a spurious (and unintended) legitimacy, and raising hackles as well as scholarly interest among observers of the German scene on both sides of the Atlantic, this particular 'historians' controversy' (*Historikerstreit*) achieved little by way of serious revision of historical interpretations of the Holocaust. [See 42, 68, 99]. Heated debates also surrounded basic policy decisions, such as concerning the foundation or slant of historical museums and exhibitions. While many West German conservatives seemed to believe that an adequate interpretation of the past, or sense of national history, would somehow anchor a fragile and problematic sense of contemporary national identity, other more liberal West Germans supported rather Habermas' notion of a more rational support of the constitution of the Federal Republic, a form of 'patriotism of the constitution'.

For all the agonising about 'overcoming the past' (*Vergangenheitsbewältigung*) in the West, and official attempts to present often distorted, black-and-white views of the past and present in the East, there is little evidence to suggest that either the debates of academics or the views promoted by governments did much to affect the sense of identity of most West and East Germans. Social and political experience, and in particular generation, seemed to be crucial factors in determining whether people saw the division of Germany as 'natural' and the two Germanies as distinct states sharing little but a common language, or as a terrible, regrettable consequence of losing the war. There was of course a fundamental asymmetry between the salience of division for West and East Germans, the former being able, quite happily, to ignore the existence of the drab and unenticing 'other Germany', while the latter were only too well aware of their effective imprisonment behind the Wall. There were also great differences with respect to generation: young West Germans in particular, with no memory of undivided Germany, tended to view it as a foreign country of little personal relevance, in contrast to older citizens with more immediate memories and links. On the other hand, young West Germans tended also to be among the least 'nationalist' of West Europeans, with a rather problematic relationship to the concept of national pride. Although treated very differently in the two Germanies, views of the past did little to help large numbers of either East or West Germans to feel proud of their respective states: rather, in different ways on each side, it was aspects of performance in the present – particularly economic performance and material satisfaction, as well as basic freedoms of expression and travel (or lack of such freedoms) – which were fundamental.

What of patterns of political culture – and in particular the intended development of democratic and socialist personalities in East and West? As far as the West is concerned, a democratic political culture shared by a majority of citizens – although not by a minority of extremists – developed in tandem with the remarkable economic recovery after the war. By the early 1960s, West Germans had apparently become what political scientists called 'fair weather democrats': so long as the system produced the material goods, they were prepared to support it. By the 1970s and 1980s, a

73

majority of West Germans were supporters of democracy in principle. This development – a result applauded of course by the western Allies, who now had a reliable friend and partner in their former enemy – was a result less of the Allies' immediate post-war re-education efforts than of the simple fact that the West German political and economic systems had actually turned out to work in practice, unlike the short-lived democracy of the Weimar Republic. [See 27, 153]. But the continuing regional and cultural diversity of the Federal Republic, as well as an often unremarked increasing ethnic diversity, renders any over-generalisation with respect to other aspects of popular political culture problematic.

As far as the GDR is concerned, developments were somewhat more wayward. Some western analysts sought to detect growing support for the system – or at least a less grumbling willingness to make the best of an unavoidable situation – in the 1960s; and perhaps even more East Germans were hopeful of a brighter future in the early Honecker years. International recognition, easier relations with and travel to the West, a degree of cultural liberalisation, a focus on social policies (such as housing) and consumer satisfaction, all seemed to augur well. But by the later 1970s, and certainly in the 1980s, the mood became more depressed. It was clear that the East German economy was faltering, that environmental pollution was reaching serious proportions and that the ageing leadership would neither deal with these issues nor contemplate the kind of political liberalisation that was on the agenda elsewhere in Eastern Europe, particularly after the accession of Gorbachev to power in the USSR in 1985. So the simplistic notion of producing good socialist personalities through a combination of changed ownership of the means of production and ideological indoctrination had clearly failed. On the other hand, patterns of political culture in the GDR did look distinctively different from those in the West.

As the often condescending and tendentious contracts drawn between *Wessis* and *Ossis* in the difficult months surrounding unification indicated, it is notoriously difficult to define, let alone explain, the differences. Some aspects were quite clearly the result of particular political circumstances. Living in a repressive regime, in which there were constant pressures to conform, and constant fears of Stasi observation and its possible consequences, many East Germans developed a form of dual life in a 'niche society'. The fear of political involvement, and difficulties with compromises made in the past, would undoubtedly continue to shadow the orientations of former East German citizens after 1990 in much the same way as many West Germans in the 1950s had tended towards a certain apoliticism. Learning how, in practice, to operate democratic procedures was also something to which those who had lived under authoritarian regimes for nearly sixty years would take some time to adjust – although the growth of indigenous, pro-democratic groups in the course of the 1980s augured well in this respect, and might even contribute new features and experiences to the democracy of united Germany. Other aspects had to do with the different socioeconomic conditions of the two Germanies. Many East Germans were critical of what they saw as the individualistic, selfish, 'elbow society' of the capitalist West. Despite the lures of material plenty for those who were successful under capitalism, they viewed with some nostalgia the lost sense of social solidarity among subjects of the former GDR. Similarly – and to a degree at odds with this point – there were assumptions about the individual autonomy of women, who were less dependent on husbands for financial and other support than in the West. The correlate here was of course greater dependence on the state (for child care facilities, subsidised food, guaranteed low-cost housing, and so on). Expectations of the paternalistic, all-providing state were probably greater as a result.

But it would be a mistake to over-generalise about the 'political culture of East Germans', for a variety of reasons. To start with, as in the West, regional, class and generation differences continued to be very important, and will certainly now need further investigation. More fundamentally, East German society was deeply divided: between those who actively sustained the regime, those who co-operated in some more minor way in its functioning, those who passively acquiesced or sought to retreat and survive, and those who, in various ways, made their disagreements felt – and suffered the consequences, minor or major. Differences between oppressors and oppressed should not be overlooked in any analysis of 'East German political culture'. But nor should they be oversimplified. Not only was East German society divided; many East Germans felt deep divisions within themselves, shades of ambivalence and doubt. These inner uncertainties were only compounded by the extraordinarily rapid, overwhelming upheavals and changes of the period from autumn 1989 to autumn 1990, when the certainties of decades were overthrown and the compromise solutions to life in a communist regime, the aspirations and strategies acquired over years, were in a matter of months rendered utterly useless.

Having briefly surveyed the changing patterns of politics, economy, society and culture in the two Germanies prior to 1989, it is time now to turn to the dramatic developments inaugurated by the East German revolution and the ultimate unification of what had, by 1990, become two very different German states.

6   The End of Two Germanies

In the autumn of 1989, a revolution took place in East Germany. As the Soviet Union renounced its claim to military intervention in the internal affairs of former satellite states, a reforming regime in Hungary decided to open its borders to Austria. Thousands of East Germans seized the opportunity to flee to the West, posing a major crisis of legitimacy – and even of basic functioning – for the GDR regime. This situation of crisis was seized upon by domestic forces for reform, spearheaded by the New Forum, which demanded legalisation. Growing protests on the streets of Leipzig and elsewhere combined with unease among the leadership of the SED at Honecker's ineffective leadership to produce, first, the replacement of Honecker by Egon Krenz, and then a series of attempted reforms from above to ward off the threat of revolution from below. In the face of ever-growing demonstrations – particularly after it had become clear, on 9 October, that protests would not be suppressed by force – concession after concession was wrung out of the regime. Finally, on 9 November 1989, the first breaches were made in the Berlin Wall, symbol of the division of Germany. In the confused weeks that followed, as waves of emigrants continued to pour westwards, and as the Communist regime collapsed among a sea of revelations of corruption, the very viability of the GDR as a separate state came into question. What had seemed unimaginable only a few months before, became the only apparent way out of the crisis: the rapid unification, first economically and then politically, of the two German states.

Less than a year after Honecker's attempted celebration of the GDR's fortieth anniversary on 7 October 1989, the GDR had ceased to exist. On 3 October 1990, the two Germanies were united in a new, enlarged, Federal Republic. How can this extraordinarily rapid, dramatic transformation be explained?

At the time of writing, there is little that could be called 'historiography': rather, discussion of such recent developments is more a combination of public debate and informed surmise. This chapter will consider certain arguments concerning the background to and manner of the collapse of the GDR and the unification of Germany. There are several aspects of relevance. First, there are the long-term implications of the previous forty years of German-German relations; secondly, there are the more immediate factors involved in the East German revolution; and finally, there is the issue of how the collapse of Communist rule was in the event resolved, and what shaped the processes of unification.

(i) West German policies towards the GDR prior to 1989

German-German relations, as we have seen, were characterised by two main phases. In the first, while lip-service was paid to the constitutional commitment to reunification with the East, West Germany's face was set very firmly westwards: western integration was pursued by Adenauer at the expense of the possibility of a united Germany. Admittedly, German unification at that time would have necessitated agreement to German neutrality, and – as the Cold War raged – the western allies were not prepared either to pre-empt any decision about the military allegiance of a future, democratically elected united German government, or to run the risk of an unprotected, ill-defended Germany being overrun by the troops of what was seen to be an aggressive, expansionist Soviet Union. Rather, Adenauer preferred the so-called 'magnet theory'. On this view, a separate West German state would ultimately be so successful, and pose such an attraction, that East Germans would be irresistibly drawn towards it. In the meantime, the legitimacy of the GDR should not be recognised, and the West should claim to speak for all Germans in the absence of East Germans' right to voice their own opinions. Some have seen, in the final collapse of the GDR in 1989–90, a vindication of Adenauer's magnet theory.

The second major phase was inaugurated by Brandt's policy of *Ostpolitik*, characterised by 'small steps' seeking to improve the real relationships between Germans in the two states, at the price of (implicitly) recognising the validity of the GDR's claims to be a separate state. At first, this was met by strong opposition from many conservatives, who saw it as totally against German national interests and even as unconstitutional. Both politically and constitutionally, however, Brandt's policies won the day, and clearly commanded considerable public support. For the following decade and a half, there was broad agreement across the political spectrum that good relations should be fostered between the two German states, in the interests of improving communication at the human level (easier travel regulations, telephone links, and so on) and improving living conditions for East Germans (favourable trade and credit agreements). Some right-wing scholars however continued to castigate *Ostpolitik* as a means of stabilising the GDR [6]. On such a view, amelioration of domestic conditions served merely to shore up the Communist regime longer than need have been the case. Others would argue, however, that the fostering of a certain consciousness of human rights, and the maintenance of all-German ties, were essential for the eventual successful outcome of movements for reform in the GDR.

What are the relative merits of these views on the contributions of West German policies towards the East? As far as Adenauer's policies are concerned, in a very distant sort of way his magnet theory might be said to have been proved broadly correct, in that, ultimately, political freedom and the promise of material plenty certainly proved highly attractive to a majority of Germans once they had any degree of choice in the matter. But what proved crucial was less the relative attractiveness of the West than the opening of the possibility of choice. And this had very little to do with Cold War fears of Soviet expansion, and a lot more to do with the ending of the Cold War, inaugurated by the Soviet Union itself. This could certainly have been neither predicted nor brought about by Adenauer's policies, and thus the claims of his magnet theory must be seen as at best rather superficial. Moreover, the sheer lapse of time from the 1950s to 1990 renders any putative thread of causation rather tenuous, as does the switch of policy under Brandt.

As far as Brandt's *Ostpolitik* is concerned, evaluation is more complex. On the one hand, it is true that the new German-German relations did contribute to the stabilisation of the GDR under Honecker. There was not the degree of material discontent in the GDR that contributed so forcefully to the power of the Solidarity movement in Poland. Even in the more difficult economic circumstances of the 1980s, the GDR was able to weather the recession more successfully than her Eastern European neighbours, largely as a result of beneficial trade relations with West Germany (and other EC countries), as well as large West German loans on favourable terms. The lack of serious mass discontent thus aided the isolation of dissenting intellectuals for a considerable time. On the other hand, the public concessions that the GDR leadership had to make with respect to human rights issues – the signing of the Helsinki Final Act, the according of a degree of public tolerance to the churches, the easing of visa restrictions for travel to the West in the 1980s – all contributed to the building up of a broader basis of grass-roots dissent in the 1980s. This was true with respect to organisational aspects (dissent was able to proliferate under the protection of the churches), and to the development of critiques of the regime (dissenters could criticise realities in the light of public proclamations). Furthermore, the mutual lowering of tensions, and willingness to engage in dialogue with the Soviet Union, was an important precondition for later subsequent negotiations with the USSR. Earlier western willingness to pursue possible avenues for mutual accommodation of interests, and to lower the degree of antagonism and hostility, should not be underestimated when trying to explain the new course adopted in East/West relations in the Gorbachev era.

Closer examination of the actual course of events leading to the collapse of the GDR will reveal that Western policies were probably less important than developments in the Soviet Union and Eastern Europe. Most would agree that the policies of Gorbachev were ultimately infinitely more important in bringing about the end of the division of Germany than were those of Adenauer or Brandt. As in all revolutions, however, causation is a matter of a unique combination of factors occurring at a particular historical moment. It could be argued that, on balance, the domestic developments in the GDR fostered, in part, by Brandt's policies were important elements in the way the East German revolution unfolded, once conditions were ripe. Let us look then at the more immediate factors involved in the East German revolution.

(ii) The collapse of Communist rule in East Germany

It was developments in Eastern Europe and the Soviet Union under the reforming leadership of Mikhail Gorbachev that proved to be vital to the collapse of the East German regime, and on which the effectiveness of domestic movements for reform was predicated.

First, the lack of Soviet intervention – indeed, the active fostering of reform movements – in other Eastern European states was a crucial factor. In particular, the willingness to allow a reformist regime in Hungary to start dismantling its fortified border – the 'Iron Curtain' – with neighbouring Austria was the final precipitant of the East German revolution. For thousands of East German holidaymakers in Hungary in the summer of 1989 took the opportunity to flee westwards, while other East Germans at home, watching scenes on television of the joyful arrival of their compatriots in the freedom of the West, decided to seek refuge in West German embassies in Prague and Warsaw. It was the renewed haemorrhage of skilled labour – not seen since the erection of the Berlin Wall in 1961 – which revealed the hollowness of the SED's claim to legitimacy and initiated the ultimate collapse of Communist rule in the GDR.

81

As far as GDR politics were concerned, there were two important sets of longer- and short-term implications of the changed climate in Eastern Europe under Gorbachev. First, Gorbachev's reforming views had for some time given general aspirations as well as specific slogans and policies to dissenters in the GDR, who nourished hopes of the introduction of restructuring and openness (*perestroika* and *glasnost*) into the neo-Stalinist style of 'actually existing socialism' under Honecker. It was these dissenters who, in the face of the escalating crisis of refugees fleeing the country, came out onto the streets demanding liberalisation and democratisation at home, such that citizens of the GDR would want to stay and work for a better future in their own country. Against the regime's clearly spurious claims to represent the people, increasing numbers of demonstrators now proclaimed that '*We* are the People' – and 'We are staying here'.

Secondly, the changed direction of Soviet communism had, from the mid-1980s onwards, introduced new elements of discussion and incipient factionalism into the previously well-disciplined SED. Given Honecker's age and the uncertainty of the succession question, this was highly significant. In the event, critiques of Honecker's inflexible responses to the mounting crises of the summer and early autumn of 1989 among Politburo members, along with Gorbachev's clear lack of support for Honecker, signalled when he visited on the occasion of the fortieth anniversary celebrations, directly led to Honecker's downfall and replacement by Egon Krenz on 18 October 1989. (Krenz, in fact, was something of a second choice: more in line with Gorbachev's reforming views was Hans Modrow, First Secretary in Dresden, but not as yet a member of the Politburo and therefore ineligible as a candidate.) Thus Gorbachev provided both the indirect stimulation and the direct impetus for a switch to a more reforming leadership in the GDR. Moreover, the greater degree of debate and variegation of opinion among SED members – including regional and local leaders – played a role in the range of official responses to domestic unrest. Very important in this connection was the decision to desist from the use of force to repress unrest – the renouncing of any massacre along the lines of the Chinese suppression of pro-democracy demonstrators in Tiananmen Square earlier in the year. The emphasis on non-violence among protesters aided the willingness to engage in dialogue on the part of certain authorities, and contributed to the – by no means inevitable – 'gentle' manner in which the revolution unfolded.

Finally, it was the USSR's – somewhat hesitating – willingness to relinquish the GDR to the West, and to put an end to the Cold War, which was the major precondition for the denouement of the East German revolution in the unification of the two Germanies in 1990.

(iii)   The unification of the two Germanies

Unification with – or takeover by – West Germany was very far from the minds of most of those courageous individuals who spearheaded the movement for reform in the autumn of 1989. Rather, groups such as New Forum wanted to initiate discussions of shortcomings in the GDR with a view to improving conditions: they wanted free elections, freedom of the press and media, freedom to travel, freedom from the oppression of the Stasi, economic reforms, greater sensitivity to environmental matters, a reduction in militarism. Despite this list, there was no agreed set of specific policies on particular issues: there was rather the desire simply that important issues should be subject to public debate and ultimately democratic decision-making by a responsible and accountable government. The ideal of most was a form of (often only vaguely defined) democratic socialism.

Yet what they got, within a year, was unification with the capitalist West, on the terms of the West. How did this come about? What roles were played by different individuals – particularly the 'unification Chancellor', Helmut Kohl – and by different social, economic and political factors?

Kohl narrowly evaded a rather poor historical write-up. His chancellorship had been characterised by navigation around a series of scandals, such as the Flick affair, and political banana-skins, such as his mismanagement of the US President's visit to SS graves at Bitburg; the popularity of Kohl's party and the prospects for re-election of a CDU/DSU/FDP coalition had been somewhat reduced by a combination of threats from the far-right (the rise of the Republicans) and the decline of the FDP alongside, for a while, rising relative popularity of the SDP and continuing electoral support for the Greens. The West German party system had seemed to be subject to a certain new fragmentation and a degree of voter disaffection and volatility, while the Chancellor had at times seemed less than agile at handling problems. Yet Kohl was saved from an unfavourable historical verdict by having the German question thrust upon him, and by seizing the opportunity with considerable astuteness and strength. His energetic intervention – and his refusal to offer unconditional economic aid at first – clearly shaped the way in which the problems consequent on collapse of Communist rule in the GDR were resolved. But these problems were not of Kohl's making; and others too played a role in the manner of their resolution. The most important factor which led to the unification of the two Germanies was economic: the GDR simply was not viable as a separate state once it was open to the competition of the capitalist West, while the latter was placed under intolerable strain by the influx of migrants from the East.

Even after the opening of the Berlin Wall on 9 November – the most symbolic concession of the would-be reformist Krenz regime, designed to symbolize the completeness of the *Wende*, or change, in domestic politics – GDR citizens continued to leave for the West, seeking better material prospects for the future. While at the end of November 1989 most observers were amazed at Kohl's 'Ten-point Plan' for closer co-operation, and eventually confederation, leading towards political unification of the two Germanies, by February 1990 it was widely accepted that the GDR could not survive for long on its own. Continued loss of skilled labour, disruptions of production, collapse of local administration, acute social and psychological problems, amounted to a very grave crisis indeed in the GDR. The round-table government under Prime Minister Hans Modrow, which was formed after the SED renounced its constitutional claim to power in December 1989, was unable to deal with these escalating problems. But nor was the coalition government formed after the March 1990 elections – the outcome of which had been heavily influenced by the influx of West German assistance for chosen parties, and the promise of Deutschmarks more speedily in the event of a victory for conservative forces sponsored by Kohl. Far from turning the East German economy around, the currency union in July 1990 only exacerbated rising unemployment and short-time working, increased bankruptcies, reduced standards of living and heightened uncertainty about the future. Negotiations about the unification treaty were clouded too by an atmosphere of suspicion and distrust on the East German side, connected very closely with the issue of complicity with Stasi activities and the problem of what to do with the Stasi records. Under these circumstances, it was scarcely surprising that experienced West German bureaucrats should make all the running, while East German politicians had little with which to bargain in the negotiations for a balanced unification treaty. Given the mounting domestic crises, even the date of unification, 3 October, was brought forward to the earliest possible moment after the resolution of external aspects of unification.

This was the other major factor involved in unification and the regaining – for the first time since the defeat of Hitler – of full sovereignty for Germany. And, as with the origins of the East German revolution, a key role was played in the resolution of the German question by the attitudes of the Soviet Union. After early prevarication on the issue of military allegiance of a united Germany, the effective collapse in any event of the Warsaw Pact meant that the USSR had to accept united Germany's membership in a NATO which would, in the post-Cold War era, redefine its role. In the process of negotiations, Germany had to make significant concessions by way of both domestic troop reductions, and considerable financial and technical aid to the ailing Soviet economy, as well as paying for the removal of Soviet troops from the soil of the former GDR by 1994. These negotiations proved more complex than those with the western powers. The three western war-time allies – the USA, Britain and France – relatively readily gave formal approval (even if tinged by residues of anti-German sentiment and ill-founded fears of German aggression on the part of some politicians) to the unification of the two Germanies in peace and freedom. The agreements reached in the so-called '2+4' talks were ratified finally by the Conference on Security and Co-operation in Europe (CSCE), paving the way for formal unification ceremonies at midnight on 2/3 October 1990. Chancellor Kohl soon reaped his political reward: in the first all-German general elections, in December 1990, he was resoundingly elected Chancellor of united Germany.

As with the initial division of Germany, so the eventual unification of the two Germanies was very much a result of, and essentially predicated on, major changes in the international situation. The Cold War precipitated the initial division of Germany; the end of the Cold War permitted unification of what had, after four decades, become two very different Germanies. The end of division was not a simple matter of *re*unification, but rather the creation of something very new, with its own unique characteristics and problems.

The Germany of 1990 was very different from the Germany which had been divided after the Second World War. It occupied a place in a rather different, and rapidly changing, European system, and would have to define a new role within the processes of European integration which were already underway. The effective takeover of the polluted and underdeveloped eastern provinces, with legal entanglements and property disputes delaying processes of privatisation, rendered the economy of united Germany – at least in the short term – relatively less powerful, its currency less sound, its role within the European Community more problematic than that of the former West Germany alone. The new, undivided and sovereign Germany would also have to define its political and military role in the wider international system. The Gulf War of spring 1991 revealed to the world that the Germans had perhaps learned their pacifist lessons too well: German aid for the United Nations forces in the military conflict against Iraq's Saddam Hussein was belated and hedged with domestic debate and ambivalence. A major political issue of 1991 became that of amendments to the German constitution allowing wider use of German military force. At the same time, with the effective disbanding of the Warsaw Pact and end of the Cold War, the role of NATO itself – and Germany's place in it – would have to be redefined.

On the domestic front, too, there were major economic and social problems. The relatively unprotected and rapid transition from a planned to a market economy in the East, with currency union on the politically advantageous but economically disastrous one-to-one basis, soon produced rising unemployment and short-term working for an ever-growing proportion of the population. Reorganisation and reconstruction of local government in the five new *Länder* was characterised by a degree of bureaucratic chaos running counter to all generalisations about German efficiency. Escalating costs of reconstruction led to belated, but snowballing, subsidies from the Bonn government, simply to keep the new provinces functioning. And for the former citizens of the GDR themselves, the strains of rising unemployment were compounded by uncertainties over such matters as subsidised housing, or the continued existence of childcare facilities. This volatile combination of factors in a society undergoing rapid transformation gave rise to a range of individual, psychological ills; and social tensions often also led, for some, to political extremism and racial hostility. Violent attacks on ethnic minorities increased alarmingly in the early months of 1991. The unification of the two Germanies was clearly going to be a more problematic affair than had at first appeared, in the euphoria following the fall of the Wall.

In the early part of the twentieth century, Germany had been characterised by domestic instability and foreign expansionism. The Second World War brought two new superpowers into Europe, and dramatically altered the parameters of the 'German question'. Following the defeat of Hitler, the division of Germany under the domination of the superpowers had for forty years seemed to provide some sort of solution to the German problem. In the closing decade of the twentieth century, the parameters began to shift again. As so often over the centuries, the boundaries of 'Germany', in the essentially unstable system of states in central Europe, had been redrawn. And yet at the same time, with the effective retreat of the superpowers and the processes of closer European economic integration and political co-operation, the role of the European nation states themselves was being redefined. The Germany which was unified in 1990 would have to define a new role, in a new Europe and a changing world, based on the lessons and shaped by the experiences of the recent past. It is time now to reflect more generally on interpretations of the two Germanies which together were to constitute the new Germany of 1990.

7 Conclusions

One of the most interesting features of the two Germanies is that they were both founded as conscious attempts to create new – and very different – forms of society and politics on the basis of a discredited and discarded past. The division of defeated Nazi Germany, and the foundation of almost diametrically opposed, capitalist and communist systems, is an experiment perhaps unparalleled in history. The record of their development is at the same time the test of that experiment: it is to a certain extent the test of social and political theory in practice.

Given the ultimate outcome – the unification of Germany on West German terms – one must obviously pose the questions: why did West Germany appear to be the 'winner'; and what went wrong with the GDR? A state ostensibly founded on the desire to create a classless, egalitarian society, in which all human beings would be emancipated from the oppressions of capitalism, and which, moreover, would in the German case also mark a total break with the Nazi past, had instead developed into a dictatorship of party and bureaucracy, failing even to satisfy physical, material and environmental needs, let alone human desires for freedom and potential for creativity and self-development.

Let us take the problem of the GDR first. The answer to the question of 'what went wrong?' depends partly on one's view of the Marxist ideology on which communist states were premised, and partly on historical analysis of the actual course of events. Arguably, the underpinning ideology (or would-be 'scientific' theory of society) was hopelessly wrong in the first place. But as a set of beliefs and ideals (rather than a science) Marxism, like Christianity, has provided a powerful vision and a set of morally informed goals, and, whatever one makes of the various developments of Marxist theory, it must be the task of the historian to analyse why certain ideals were so distorted or perverted in practice. Equally, whatever one makes of the final collapse of the GDR, it is important to ask what was 'achieved' – in the light of certain ideals – in the forty years of its existence.

Various arguments have been put forward on these matters. Some see the basic problems in the earlier attempt to establish a communist state in a relatively backward country, namely Russia. The forced rapid industrialisation, the concentration on heavy industry and collectivisation of agriculture, the political oppressions partly (but not entirely) explicable in terms of the supposedly 'necessary' imposition of deeply unpopular policies, the attempt to develop socialism in one country in the face of a hostile world – all these features contributed to the phenomenon of Stalinism and, following the dreadful experiences of the USSR under attack by Nazi Germany, the determination to ensure that the character of German politics was changed fundamentally. The imposition of a Stalinist regime in the Soviet zone of Germany, and its development again in a hostile world context when the fear of overt attack or covert undermining from the West was very real, together should explain the peculiar system of oppression developed in the GDR.

Such a view focusses primarily on the supposedly inappropriate conditions in which the experiment – in itself valid – was attempted. Others would however see the experiment itself as fundamentally misguided. On this view, for example, a centrally planned economy, with state ownership of the means of production (even if in the name of the people) could never work. Economically, without a free market to determine the balance of supply and demand, there would be too many dislocations and inefficiencies to satisfy people's material needs and desires. Politically, the power of the state to determine what was deemed to be for the good of the people would condemn the latter to a permanent state of immaturity, to a 'subject' rather than 'citizen' status. Socially, the importance of power and privilege would ensure that there never could be a genuinely classless society. On such a view, the ideology on which the experiment was based was mistaken from the very start.

Others would insert into the debate the question of positive 'achievements' of the GDR, irrespective of its ultimate collapse. Even if the greater relative equality of women with men in the GDR is dismissed as a greater equality of misery rather than anything approaching emancipation, some of the social policies which enhanced women's freedom of choice (particularly the generous child care provision) are pointed to as factors not to be ignored in a final balance sheet. So too are the subsidised rents and food prices, the guaranteed housing and employment, the provision of adequate pensions, and a universally available health service – even if, again, these are qualified in terms of rather minimal standards or a low quality of life. More ethereally, some have praised a certain social solidarity among people subjected to common constraints and pressures, in contrast to the materialist, individualist 'elbow society' of the capitalist west, and have valued the qualities of GDR cultural, moral and religious life.

We shall return to the wider implications of these debates in a moment. But it is important now to consider the case of West Germany. Why was it that democracy in the Federal Republic was, in contrast to its Weimar predecessor, so stable? A number of factors appear to be important.

The settlement after the Second World War, as far as the western zones were concerned, contrasted markedly with the treatment meted out in the Versailles Treaty of 1919. Although in some respects harsher (division, loss of sovereignty), the early commitment of the western Allies to economic reconstruction on firm foundations constituted a major, indeed fundamental, difference. And it was on the early spectacular success of the West German economy, as well as its commitment to Western integration on the lines of the American conception of the post-war world order, that the stability of West German democracy in the early years was based. As far as more domestic factors were concerned, constitutional provisions (the outlawing of anti-democratic parties, the 5 per cent hurdle) were of some importance. But probably more important was the way in which the structures of West German political and economic life gained the support and commitment of key elite groups. It was not only politicians who came to support the new system in principle: it was also the leaders of business and industry, as well as the trade unions, who – for all the differences over degrees of co-determination or social partnership – found that the corporatist structures actually worked and helped to protect their interests, at least within a rapidly growing economy. With the passage of time, as West Germany became a respected partner in the western alliances, and as a generation came to maturity who took democratic politics for granted, the system was sufficiently well-anchored to weather greater economic difficulties. It was also sufficiently secure to cope with challenges from political extremists at the margins, and to conduct with a modicum of tolerance an at times acerbic public debate over its relations with its past. [For more detailed discussion of contrasts with the Weimar Republic, see 48].

As far as the outcome in 1989–90 is concerned, however, there are at least two notes of caution which must be struck with respect to the apparent 'winner' of the historical contest. For one thing, at the close of the 1980s it was less that capitalism 'won' than that communism collapsed, for a range of factors more related to events in the eastern bloc than the West. For another, with respect to criticisms of Marx's ideas, neither East German 'communism' nor West German 'capitalism' were in actuality anything like the pure types described by Karl Marx. Bureaucratic state socialism in innumerable respects perverted the ideals embodied in Marx's vision of communism. Meanwhile the capitalism of the late twentieth century was so modified, with so many safeguards and welfare provisions, so much state intervention, that the worst effects of a free market were mitigated. History had simply moved on from the period in which Marx worked out his ideas – and history did not thus constitute any real test of Marx's global theories (which were in any event riddled with ambiguities which cannot be explored here).

Moreover, despite the appearance of having 'won' the historical contest (not least in the terms of unification in 1990), and despite its very real achievements in terms of economic productivity and democratic stability, West Germany also has been evaluated in the light of differing criteria. Its predominantly conservative complexion has provoked a range of radical critiques. Crass materialism has consistently been criticised, from the 1950s onwards; the reincorporation of former Nazis, and the difficulties in coming to terms with the Nazi past, have been subjected to much controversy; the reproduction of social inequalities, the hostile treatment of ethnic minorities or foreign workers, the relative poverty and neglect of many pensioners, have aroused criticism. But a fundamental difference is that such criticisms can be raised – and fought out – within the terms and parameters of the democratic political system itself. Pressure groups and parties can seek to change the conditions they criticise. Furthermore, West German democracy has enjoyed considerable good fortune in being based in a powerful, and well-run, economy, where economic growth and increased prosperity for all have served to disguise the persistence of relative social inequalities. Despite all the very real problems of a social market form of capitalism – the business cycle, the existence of unemployment, inequality of life chances, the persistence of poverty alongside extraordinary wealth – for many the prospects for personal advance and a high standard of living have outweighed the risks associated with such a system.

It is clear that any historical analysis of the two Germanies will easily be tempted into the shoals of moral and political evaluation. But the task of the historian is essentially to analyse and explain, not to evaluate. Stepping outside the self-understandings of political actors in the drama of the two Germanies, can we develop any general conclusions on the basis of the analysis presented in the preceding chapters?

First, no society can be viewed purely in self-contained terms. Both Germanies can only be understood as part of a wider international system – political, military and economic. Their relative successes and failures in different spheres have much to do with the wider systems of which they were a part and in which they played distinctive roles. The GDR's longevity, and ultimate end, had, very obviously, much to do with the interests and capacities of the Soviet Union. Its relative economic success also had not a little to do with its special relationship with the Federal Republic. But equally, the success of West German democracy had much to do with its economic success, predicated initially on American rebuilding after the war and premised further on a developing role in both world markets and the European Community. Neither Germany can be explained purely in terms of its own particular political and economic system, without reference to the wider conditions of Europe and the world. So neither system, in the abstract, can be adjudicated solely on its record in its particular part of divided Germany.

Secondly, and partly related to this, the kind of global comparison of systems that used to be popular should be abandoned in favour of a more differentiated approach to analysis of specific aspects and areas. Catch-all concepts such as 'capitalism', 'communism', 'totalitarianism' will not serve to unlock the secrets of detailed historical developments. 'Capitalism' was not simply associated with successful democracy in the Weimar Republic or the Third Reich; its political supporters still have to explain why market economies are sometimes, but not always, connected with political freedoms. Nor is the picture any easier with respect to the allegedly intrinsic economic shortcomings of communism, or the repression associated with notions of 'totalitarianism'. For example, there is little point in appealing to material discontent as a key causal factor in explaining the origins of the East German revolution, since it had been insufficient to upset the political system over the previous forty years. Similarly, the use of force as a means of controlling the population varied over time: to appeal to 'repression' as an unchanging factor is again to miss many nuances and variations. Rather, unique combinations of factors under changing circumstances must be considered to explain particular eventuations.

Certain elements of such a multifaceted approach to the two Germanies have been suggested above. With respect to West Germany, distinctive features of its social market economy and constitution, under favourable international circumstances, aided the development of a relatively stable democracy characterised by widespread, if not universal, material affluence, and a degree of critical debate. For all its acknowledged shortcomings, the West German system – for a variety of reasons – appeared to work. With respect to East Germany, a peculiar combination of changing domestic factors produced a certain stability over forty years – a record not to be forgotten in the light of the GDR's ultimate collapse. In the 1950s, a combination of repression and the exclusion of domestic dissent laid the foundations for the 'established phase' which followed the construction of the Wall and the achievement of international recognition after *Ostpolitik*. During the 1960s and 1970s, intellectual dissent was relatively easily isolated or exiled, and modest rates of economic growth produced at least quiescence on the part of the majority of the population, at a time when there appeared to be few viable alternatives. The regime's experiment with a greater latitude of toleration *vis-à-vis* the church from the late 1970s even gave some cause to hope for a degree of liberalisation in time. Increasing pressure for change from within was fuelled by the accession of Mikhail Gorbachev to power in the Soviet Union, with the introduction of major reforms there and elsewhere in Eastern Europe – which were, however, resisted by Honecker and the old guard leadership. East German hopes for reform were dashed when the rapid proliferation of domestic dissent gave rise to increased use of force and suppression on the part of a rattled regime in the later 1980s. The opening of the Iron Curtain between Austria and Hungary in the summer of 1989 came at a time of peculiar domestic lability in the GDR. The decisive factors affecting the ultimate outcome were, on the one hand, for the first time since 1961 the possibility of flight to the West for the previously passive majority, combined with, on the other, the refusal on the part of the Soviet Union to countenance or support the use of force in the suppression of domestic movements for reform. The result, as we now know, was to be the end of the GDR.

It has not been possible in this brief compass to do more than touch on the many aspects and approaches relevant to interpreting the two Germanies. There are moreover many areas which now warrant more serious historical attention, particularly with respect to the GDR, the collapse of which has transformed the conditions for scholarly research. But this is a very recent past, analysis of which has political implications in the present, and there will inevitably be new constraints and considerations affecting the character of research. Following unification, the availability of new material is leading to new perspectives and new debates on the tangled, contentious histories of the two Germanies. The extraordinary, unparalleled experiment of founding two such very different states and societies, a capitalist democracy and a communist state, on the soil of defeated Nazi Germany, and then of engaging in the unprecedented process of subsequently recombining them, is certain to remain a subject of lively academic controversy as well as political engagement. For all the apparent 'normality' over recent decades of at least West German history, it seems as if, once again, the Germans have been following their own peculiar historical path, their German *Sonderweg*.

Select Bibliography

This bibliography contains those works referred to in the text and other, mostly recent, important references. A few collections of documents and other primary sources, but not works of creative literature, have also been listed. A number of texts in German have been included, particularly with respect to the later years of the GDR or comparing aspects of the two Germanies. It should be noted that this bibliography reflects the state of publication up to 1990. It is likely that the field will see a rapid development with, in particular, the opening up of new opportunities for research on East German history.

Those English-language texts which might form particularly useful components of a short bibliography for teaching purposes have been marked with an asterisk. The works thus denoted will guide interested readers towards further reading on particular topics.

[1] W. Abelshauser, *Wirtschaftsgeschichte der Bundesrepublik Deutschland, 1945–1980* (Frankfurt: Suhrkamp, 1983).

[2] J. Backer, *The Decision to Divide Germany* (Durham, N.C.: Duke University Press, 1978).

[3] R. Bahro, *The Alternative in Eastern Europe* (London: New Left Books, 1978). Important East German dissident text.

*[4] M. Balfour, *West Germany: A Contemporary History* (London: Croom Helm, 1982). Detailed narrative history of West Germany up to the early 1980s.

[5] A. Baring, *Uprising in East Germany* (New York: Cornell University Press, 1972). Classic account of the uprising of 17 June 1953, stressing its lack of leadership and loss of momentum even before Soviet troops came to put it down.

[6]   D. Bark and D. Gress, *A History of West Germany*, 2 vols
        (Oxford: Basil Blackwell, 1989). Right-wing block-buster,
        marred by Cold War prejudices.

[7]   T. Baylis, *The Technical Intelligentsia and the East German
        Elite* (Berkeley: University of California Press, 1974). Impor-
        tant study of the lack of political cohesion and variety of
        attitudes among the East German technical intelligentsia, who
        did not form a potential 'counter-elite' as in Ludz' thesis.

[8]   J. Becker, *Hitler's Children* (London: Panther, 1977). Account
        of the Baader-Meinhof gang, terrorist heirs of the generation
        which had sustained Nazism.

[9]   W. Behr, *Bundesrepublik Deutschland – Deutsche Demokrat-
        ische Republik: Systemvergleich* (Stuttgart: Kohlhammer,
        1979). Typical West German attempt at 'comparison of
        systems'.

[10]   W. Benz (ed.), *Die Bundesrepublik Deutschland*, 3 vols
        (Frankfurt: Fischer, 1983). Useful collection of articles on
        aspects of West Germany's politics, economy, society and
        culture.

[11]   V. Berghahn, *The Americanisation of West German Industry
        1945–73* (Leamington Spa: Berg, 1986). Sees key changes in
        attitudes of German industrialists with the generation change
        of the 1960s.

[12]   V. Berghahn, *Modern Germany* (Cambridge: Cambridge
        University Press, 2nd edn, 1987). Good textbook for
        the longer-term development of twentieth-century German
        economy, society and politics, from Imperial Germany to
        the Federal Republic. Thin on the GDR.

[13]   V. Berghahn and D. Karsten, *Industrial Relations in West
        Germany* (Oxford: Berg, 1987). Clear account of current
        industrial relations law and practice, followed by analysis
        of the historical roots of the current framework. Interesting
        concluding discussion.

*[14]   K. von Beyme and H. Zimmermann (eds), *Policymaking in
        the German Democratic Republic* (Aldershot: Gower, 1984).
        Contains important essays on a range of topics, particularly
        the long piece by Zimmermann.

[15]   K. von Beyme, *The Political System of the Federal Republic
        of Germany* (Aldershot: Gower, 1984). Solid textbook, marred
        by poor English translation.

[16]   S. Bulmer and W. Paterson, *The Federal Republic of Germany
        and the European Community* (London: Allen & Unwin,
        1987). Explores West Germany's unique position in a
        variety of aspects of European integration since the early
        post-war years.

98

[17]   C. Burdick *et al.* (eds), *Contemporary Germany: Politics and Culture* (Boulder, Colorado: Westview Press, 1984).

[18]   R. Burns and W. van der Will, *Protest and Democracy in West Germany: Extra-Parliamentary Opposition and the Democratic Agenda* (London: Macmillan, 1988). Explores the critical 'margins' of the 'stolid, efficient and disciplined nation': critical intellectuals, the early peace movement, student protests, feminism, citizens' initiatives, anti-nuclear protests, and the Greens.

[19]   D. Calleo, *The German Problem Reconsidered* (Cambridge: Cambridge University Press, 1978).

[20]   A. Carew, *Labour under the Marshall Plan* (Manchester: Manchester University Press, 1987). Emphasises subtle effects of Marshall Plan on the political moderation of European labour movements and spread of managerialist ideologies orientated towards enhanced productivity.

*[21] D. Childs, *The GDR: Moscow's German Ally* (London: George Allen & Unwin, 1983). Basically informative textbook on the GDR; little on dissent and religion.

*[22] D. Childs (ed.), *Honecker's Germany* (London: Allen & Unwin, 1985). Useful collection of articles on different aspects of the GDR.

[23]   D. Childs, 'Honecker's Germany', *Government and Opposition* vol. 22, 1987, pp. 78–87. Stresses material discontent of East Germans.

[24]   D. Childs, T. Baylis and M. Rueschemeyer (eds), *East Germany in Comparative Perspective* (London: Routledge, 1989).

[25]   D. Childs and J. Johnson, *West Germany: Politics and Society* (London: Croom Helm, 1981).

[26]   S. Cobler, *Law, Order and Politics in West Germany* (Harmondsworth: Penguin, 1978). Critique, from a radical perspective, of state encroachments on civil liberties by over-responding to the terrorist threat.

*[27] D. P. Conradt, *The German Polity* (London: Longman, 3rd edn, 1986. Very useful textbook.

*[28] G. Craig, *The Germans* (Harmondsworth: Penguin, 1978). Quirky, idiosyncratic, provocative and highly readable account of aspects of German life and culture over the centuries.

[29]   H. Dähn, *Konfrontation oder Kooperation? Das Verhältnis von Staat und Kirche in der SBZ/DDR 1945–1980* (Opladen: Westdeutscher Verlag, 1982). Detailed account of church/state relations. Lacks a social history dimension.

[30]   R. Dahrendorf, *Society and Democracy in Germany* (London: Weidenfeld and Nicolson, 1968). Classic analysis, provocative

hypotheses, still well worth engaging with.

[31]   *DDR-Handbuch* (Köln: Verlag Wissenschaft und Politik). Invaluable reference work; several editions.

*[32]   M. Dennis, *German Democratic Republic* (London: Pinter, 1988). Clear, well-researched and useful textbook.

[33]   Deutsches Institut für Wirtschaftsforschung Berlin (ed.), *Handbuch DDR-Wirtschaft* (Hamburg: Rowohlt, 4th edn, 1984). Useful compendium on East German economy.

[34]   *Deutschland-Archiv.* Important periodical, invaluable for GDR studies.

[35]   H. Döring and G. Smith (eds), *Party Government and Political Culture in Western Germany* (New York: St. Martin's Press, 1982).

[36]   A. Dorpalen, *German History in Marxist Perspective: The East German Approach* (London: I. B. Tauris, 1985).

[37]   R. Ebsworth, *Restoring Democracy in Germany* (London: Stevens and Sons Ltd., 1960). Very favourable picture of the 'British contribution'.

[38]   G. Eckart, *So sehe ick die Sache. Protokolle aus der DDR* (Köln: Kiepenhauer and Witsch, 1984).

*[39]   L. Edinger, *West German Politics* (New York: Columbia University Press, 1986). Useful textbook, from an American perspective.

*[40]   G. E. Edwards, *GDR Society and Social Institutions* (London: Macmillan, 1985). Rather rosy picture, but useful information.

[41]   K. Ehring and M. Dallwitz, *Schwerter zu Pflugscharen: Friedensbewegung in der DDR* (Hamburg: Rowohlt, 1982). Important source for the early stages of East German peace initiatives.

[42]   Richard J. Evans, *In Hitler's Shadow* (London: I. B. Tauris, 1989). On the West German 'historians' dispute'.

[43]   C. Fitzgibbon, *Denazification* (London: Michael Joseph, 1969).

[44]   T. Forster, *The East German Army* (London: George Allen & Unwin, 5th edn, 1980). Emphasizes all-pervasive militarisation of GDR.

[45]   M. Freund, *From Cold War to Ostpolitik* (London: Oswald Wolff, 1972).

[46]   R. Fritsch-Bournazel, *Confronting the German Question* (Oxford: Berg, 1988).

[47]   M. Fulbrook, *A Concise History of Germany* (Cambridge: Cambridge University Press, 1990). Long sweep of German history: Ch. 7 provides a brief account of the two Germanies.

*[48]   M. Fulbrook, *Germany 1918–1990: The Divided Nation* (London: Fontana, 1991). A more extended interpretation of the dynamics of recent German history.

[49]   G. Gaus, *Wo Deutschland liegt* (Munich: dtv, 1986). Classic analysis of the GDR's 'niche society', by a former 'permanent representative' of the Bonn government in the GDR.

[50]   *GDR Monitor*. Useful periodical on East Germany; considerable emphasis on literary and cultural matters.

[51]   J. Gimbel, *The American Occupation of Germany: Politics and the Military, 1945–49* (Stanford: Stanford University Press, 1968).

[52]   G.-J. Glaessner, *Die Andere Deutsche Republik* (Opladen: Westdeutscher Verlag, 1989). Detailed and informative textbook on the GDR, published on the eve of its demise.

[53]   R. Goeckel, *The Lutheran Church and the East German State* (Ithaca: Cornell University Press, 1990).

*[54]   A. Grosser, *Germany In Our Time* (London: Pall Mall Press, 1971). Intriguing account by a French observer; particularly good on early post-war period.

[55]   H. Haftendorn, *Security and Detente: Conflicting Priorities in German Foreign Policy* (New York: Praeger, 1985).

*[56]   K. Hardach, *The Political Economy of Germany in the Twentieth Century* (Berkeley: University of California Press, 1980).

[57]   R. Havemann, *An Alienated Man* (London: Davis-Poynter, 1973). The views of an important East German dissident of the 1960s and 1970s (died 1982).

[58]   A. Hearndon (ed.), *The British in Germany: Educational Reconstruction after 1945* (London: Hamish Hamilton, 1978).

[59]   A. Hearndon (ed.), *Education in the Two Germanies* (Oxford: Basil Blackwell, 1974).

[60]   A. Heidenheimer, *Adenauer and the CDU* (The Hague, 1960).

[61]   H. Heitzer, *GDR: An Historical Outline* (Dresden: Verlag Zeit im Bild, 1981). Official East German history of GDR in English.

[62]   G. Helwig, *Frau und Familie* (Köln: Verlag Wissenschaft und Politik, 2nd edn, 1987). Informative profile of the position of women and the family in the two Germanies.

[63]   G. Helwig and D. Urban (eds), *Kirchen und Gesellschaft in beiden deutschen Staaten* (Köln: Verlag Wissenschaft und Politik, 1987). Collection of essays and documents on religion in the two Germanies.

101

[64]   R. Henkys (ed.), *Die evangelischen Kirchen in der DDR* (Munich: Chr. Kaiser Verlag, 1982). Contains very useful essays on East German Protestantism.

[65]   R. Henrich, *Der vormundschaftliche Staat* (Hamburg: Rowohlt, 1990). Important late dissident analysis of the GDR, first published in the spring of 1989.

[66]   D. R. Herspring, *East German Civil-military Relations: the Impact of Technology, 1949–72* (New York: Praeger, 1973). Finds no development in the GDR of a body of independent military experts as in USSR. Important contribution to the debate on the relations between technical expertise and political control in the GDR.

[67]   J. Hirsch, 'Developments in the political system of West Germany since 1945', in R. Scase (ed.), *The State in Western Europe* (London: Croom Helm, 1980). An occasionally impenetrable analysis from a Marxist point of view.

[68]   *Historikerstreit* (Munich: Piper, 1987). Collection of important original contributions to the 'historians' dispute'.

[69]   M. Hogan, *The Marshall Plan* (Cambridge: Cambridge University Press, 1987).

[70]   G. Holzweissig, *Militärwesen in der DDR* (Berlin: Holzapfel, 1985). Readable, illustrated and informative account of attempted, but ultimately unsuccessful, militarisation of life in the GDR, from the army, through the economy, to the workers' militia groups.

[71]   E. Honecker, *Der Sturz*, ed. R. Andert and W. Herzberg (Berlin and Weimar: Aufbau Verlag, 1990). Honecker's reflections after his fall, sensitively elicited through a series of interviews.

[72]   W. Hülsberg, *The German Greens: A Social and Political Profile* (London: Verso, 1988).

[73]   I. Jeffries and M. Melzer, *The East German Economy* (London: Croom Helm, 1987).

[74]   E. Jesse (ed.), *Bundesrepublik Deutschland und Deutsche Demokratische Republik: Die beiden deutschen Staaten im Vergleich* (Berlin: Colloquium Verlag, 3rd edn, 1982).

[75]   P. Katzenstein, *Policy and Politics in West Germany: The Growth of a Semi-sovereign State* (Philadelphia: Temple University Press 1987). Explores lack of major policy shifts despite changes in political administrations, with discussion and documentation of: economic management; industrial relations; social welfare; migrant workers; administrative reform; and university reform.

[76]   P. Katzenstein (ed.), *Industry and Politics in West Germany* (Ithaca: Cornell University Press, 1989).

[77] O. Kirchheimer, 'Germany: the vanishing opposition' in R. A. Dahl (ed.), *Political Oppositions in Western Democracies* (New Haven: Yale University Press, 1966). Points to the convergence of conservative and social-democratic parties in West Germany by the early 1960s.

[78] *Kleines Politisches Wörterbuch* (Berlin: Dietz-Verlag, 3rd edn, 1978). Official East German views on various political topics.

[79] C. Klessmann, *Die doppelte Staatsgründung* (Göttingen: Vandenhoek and Ruprecht, 1982). Excellent collection of documents, useful discussions and guide to further literature.

[80] C. Klessmann, *Zwei Staaten, eine Nation: Deutsche Geschichte 1955–70* (Göttingen: Vandenhoek and Ruprecht, 1988). More of the same, for the subsequent period.

[81] P. Ködderitsch and L. Müller, *Rechtsextremismus in der DDR* (Göttingen: Lamuv Verlag, 1990). Study of right-wing extremism in the GDR, even before it became more evident in 1989–90.

[82] E. Kolinsky (ed.), *The Greens in West Germany* (Oxford: Berg, 1989).

*[83] E. Kolinsky, *Parties, Opposition and Society in West Germany* (London: Croom Helm, 1984).

[84] E. Kolinsky, *Women in West Germany* (Oxford: Berg, 1989).

[85] H. Königsdorf, *Adieu DDR* (Hamburg: Rowohlt, 1990). 'Protocols' of former GDR citizens on the demise of their state.

[86] J. Krejci, *Social Structure in Divided Germany* (London: Croom Helm, 1976).

*[87] H. Krisch, *The German Democratic Republic* (Boulder, Colorado: Westview Press, 1985). Informative textbook.

[88] H. Krisch, *German Politics under Soviet Occupation* (New York: University of Columbia Press, 1984).

[89] F. Kroh (ed.), *'Freiheit ist immer Freiheit . . .' Die Andersdenkenden in der DDR* (Berlin: Ullstein, 1988). Dissident movements in 1980s GDR.

[90] W. Laqueur, *Germany Today: A Personal Report* (London: Weidenfeld and Nicolson, 1985).

[91] J. Leaman, *The Political Economy of West Germany, 1945–85* (London: Macmillan, 1988).

[92] W. Leonhard, *Child of the Revolution* (London: Collins, 1957). Autobiographical account of the early post-war years in the Soviet zone.

[93] G. Lepton and M. Melzer, *Economic Reform in East German Industry* (London: Oxford University Press, 1978). Account of

the origins, course and demise of the New Economic System, 1963–70.

[94] H. Lippmann, *Honecker and the New Politics of Europe* (New York: Macmillan, 1972).

[95] F. Loeser, *Die unglaubwürdige Gesellschaft* (Köln: Bund Verlag, 1984). Critique of East Germany by a dissident who left.

[96] P. C. Ludz, *The Changing Party Elite in East Germany* (Cambridge, Mass.: MIT Press, 1972). Important thesis suggesting a change from the totalitarianism of the 1950s to 'consultative authoritarianism' in the 1960s, in which technical expertise and qualifications supposedly began to play a greater role in the GDR.

[97] P. C. Ludz, 'East Germany: Continuity and change since Ulbricht', *Problems of Communism*, vol. 21, 1972, pp. 56–67.

[98] P. C. Ludz, *The GDR from the Sixties to the Seventies* (Harvard Center for International Affairs: Occasional Papers in International Affairs, no. 26, Nov. 1970).

[99] C. Maier, *The Unmasterable Past: History, Holocaust, and German National Identity* (Cambridge, Mass.: Harvard University Press, 1988). One of the best analyses of the West German 'historians' dispute'.

[100] A. Mallincrodt, 'WANTED: theoretical framework for GDR studies. FOR SALE: a systems/functional approach', *GDR Monitor*, no. 10 (winter 1983/4): 12–27.

[101] A. Markovits, *The Politics of West German Trade Unions: Strategies of Class and Interest Representation in Growth and Crisis* (Cambridge: Cambridge University Press, 1986). Argues importance of strong, organised labour movement to West Germany's economic prosperity and political stability; general chapters followed by case studies of I. G. Metall and other unions.

[102] B. Marshall, *The Origins of Post-war German Politics* (London: Croom Helm, 1988). Misnamed but informative local study of Hanover politics under British occupation.

[103] A. J. McAdams, *East Germany and Detente: Building Authority after the Wall* (Cambridge: Cambridge University Press, 1985).

*[104] M. McCauley, *The GDR since 1945* (London: Macmillan, 1983). Narrative history up to the early 1980s.

[105] M. McCauley, *Marxism-Leninism in the GDR* (London: Macmillan 1979).

[106] M. McCauley, *The Origins of the Cold War* (London: Longman 1983).

[107] R. Mellor, *The Two Germanies: A Modern Geography* (London: Harper and Row, 1978).

[108] A. J. Merritt and R. L. Merritt (eds), *Public Opinion in Occupied Germany: The OMGUS Surveys, 1945–49* (Urbana: University of Illinois Press, 1970). Selection from the very intriguing surveys of German public opinion carried out for the Office of Military Government (US). These and later surveys reveal continued persistence of pro-Nazi and anti-democratic attitudes among large numbers of Germans well into the late 1950s.

[109] S. Miller and H. Potthoff, *A History of German Social Democracy* (Leamington Spa: Berg, 1986). Part Two, by Susanne Miller, presents a sympathetic account of the SPD from 1945 to the early 1980s. There is also a collection of documents.

[110] G. Minnerup, 'East Germany's frozen revolution', *New Left Review* no. 132 (1982): 5–32. Informative left-wing critique of Stalinist mould of GDR.

[111] G. Minnerup, 'West Germany since the war', *New Left Review* no. 99 (1976): 3–44.

[112] A. Mitter and S. Wolle (eds), *'Ich liebe euch doch alle!' Befehle und Lageberichte des MfS, Jan.–Nov. 1989* (Berlin: BasisDruck, 1990). Highly revealing selection of documents of the East German secret police, or Stasi, including procedural commands and reports on dissident activities, in the months preceding the collapse of communist rule.

[113] N. Edwina Moreton (ed.), *Germany between East and West* (Cambridge: Cambridge University Press, 1987).

[114] J. P. Nettl, *The Eastern Zone and Soviet Policy in Germany 1945–50* (London: Oxford University Press, 1951). Still very useful.

[115] G. Neugebauer, *Partei und Staatsapparat in der DDR* (Opladen: Westdeutscher Verlag, 1978). Tries to argue that, while in the early period the SED had to intervene to gain control of the state apparatus, by the late 1970s state structures were to some degree constraining party organisation and goals.

[116] L. Niethammer, *Die Mitläuferfabrik: Die Entnazifizierung am Beispiel Bayerns* (Bonn and Berlin: Dietz Verlag, 1982). Pioneering study (and critique) of denazification in Bavaria.

[117] E. Noelle and E. P. Neumann, *Jahrbuch der Öffentlichen Meinung* (Allensbach: Verlag für Demoskopie, series, 1956–). West German public opinion surveys over the years; shows slow growth of pro-democratic attitudes, particularly from the early 1960s.

[118]   C. Offe and K. Ronge, 'Theses on the Theory of the State', in A. Giddens and D. Held (eds), *Classes, Power and Conflict* (London: Macmillan, 1982). Influential West German radical view of the state in capitalist societies. Rather gloomy prospects for parliamentary socialist parties, who are condemned to make capitalism profitable if they want to support the welfare state through high tax income.

[119]   B. Ruhm von Oppen (ed.), *Documents on Germany under Occupation, 1945–55* (London: Oxford University Press, 1955).

[120]   Robin Ostow, *Jews in Contemporary East Germany* (London: Macmillan, 1989). Suggestive protocols of interviews with a dozen East German Jews.

*[121]   W. Paterson and G. Smith (eds), *The West German Model: Perspectives on a Stable State* (London: Frank Cass, 1981).

[122]   E. Peterson, *The American Occupation of Germany* (Detroit: Wayne State University Press, 1978).

[123]   N. Pronay and K. Wilson (eds), *The Political Re-education of Germany and her Allies after World War II* (London: Croom Helm, 1985).

[124]   J. Reich, 'Reflections on becoming an East German dissident, on losing the Wall and a country', in G. Prins (ed.), *Spring in Winter. The 1989 Revolutions* (Manchester: Manchester University Press, 1990). Personal account by a founder member of New Forum.

[125]   R. Rist, *Guestworkers in Germany: The Prospects for Pluralism* (New York: Praeger, 1978).

[126]   J. Roesler, 'The black market in post-War Berlin and the methods used to counteract it', *German History* vol. 7, 1989, pp. 92–107.

[127]   J. Roesler, 'The rise and fall of the planned economy in the German Democratic Republic, 1945–89', *German History* vol. 9, 1991, pp. 46–61.

[128]   G. Sandford, *From Hitler to Ulbricht: The Communist Reconstruction of East Germany, 1945–6* (Princeton: Princeton University Press, 1983).

[129]   J. Sandford, *The Sword and the Ploughshare: Autonomous Peace Initiatives in East Germany* (London: Merlin Press/END, 1983).

[130]   G. Schabowski, *Das Politbüro* (Hamburg: Rowohlt, 1990). Intriguing set of interviews with a former member of the East German politburo who played a prominent role in the last stages of communist rule in Oct.–Nov. 1989.

[131]   C. Bradley Scharf, *Politics and Change in East Germany* (Boulder, Colorado: Westview Press, 1984).

[132] C. Schüddekopf (ed.), 'Wir sind das Volk!' (Hamburg: Rowohlt, 1990). Collection of documents on the 1989 revolution.

[133] G. Schweigler, National Consciousness in Divided Germany (London: Sage, 1975).

*[134] C. C. Schweitzer et al. (eds), Politics and Government in the Federal Republic of Germany: Basic Documents (Leamington Spa: Berg, 1984). Useful collection of documents with helpful commentaries.

[135] Harry Shaffer, Women in the Two Germanies (New York: Pergamon 1981).

[136] F. Silnitsky (ed.), Communism in Eastern Europe (Brighton: Harvester Press, 1979). Section on GDR contains useful pieces.

[137] E. Owen Smith, The West German Economy (Beckenham: Croom Helm, 1983).

*[138] G. Smith, Democracy in Western Germany (Aldershot: Gower, 3rd edn, 1986).

*[139] G. Smith, W. Paterson and Peter H. Merkl (eds), Developments in West German Politics (London: Macmillan, 1989). Some very useful essays on a wide range of topics, beyond the conventional definition of 'politics'.

*[140] K. Sontheimer and W. Bleek, The Government and Politics of East Germany (London: Hutchinson, 1975).

[141] I. Spittmann (ed.), Die SED in Geschichte und Gegenwart (Köln: Verlag Wissenschaft und Politik, 1987). Contains some very interesting essays.

[142] F. Spotts, The Churches and Politics in Germany (Middletown, Conn.: Wesleyan University Press, 1973).

[143] D. Staritz, Geschichte der DDR, 1949–1985 (Frankfurt: Suhrkamp, 1985).

[144] D. Staritz, 'Ursachen und Konsequenzen einer deutschen Revolution' in Der Fischer Welt-Almanack: Sonderband DDR (Frankfurt: Fischer, 1990).

[145] Statistisches Jahrbuch der DDR (Berlin: Staatsverlag der DDR, annually). Official statistical compendium.

[146] R. Steininger, Deutsche Geschichte 1945–61, 2 vols (Frankfurt: Fischer, 1983). Very useful collection of documents and commentary.

[147] C. Stern, Ulbricht (London: Pall Mall Press, 1965). Still useful.

[148] K. Tauber, Beyond Eagle and Swastika (Middletown, Conn.: Wesleyan University Press, 1967).

[149] James F. Tent, Mission on the Rhine: Re-education and Denazification in American-occupied Germany (Chicago:

107

University of Chicago Press, 1982).
*[150] J. K. A. Thomanek and J. Mellis (eds), *Politics, Society and Government in the German Democratic Republic: Basic Documents* (Oxford, New York, Munich: Berg, 1988).
[151] R. Tökés (ed.), *Opposition in Eastern Europe* (London: Macmillan, 1979), section on the GDR.
*[152] H. A. Turner, *The Two Germanies since 1945* (New Haven: Yale University Press, 1987). A brief, introductory narrative of the political histories of the two Germanies; rather thin on the GDR.
[153] S. Verba, 'Germany: the remaking of political culture' in L. Pye and S. Verba, *Political Culture and Political Development* (Princeton, New Jersey: Princeton University Press, 1965).
[154] I. Wallace (ed.), *East Germany*, World Bibliographical Series vol. 77 (Oxford: Clio Press, 1987). Very useful guide to the literature on East Germany up to the date of going to press. Lists 739 items under different topic headings.
[155] I. Wallace (ed.), *The GDR under Honecker, 1971–81* (Dundee: GDR Monitor Special Series, no. 1, 1981).
[156] I. Wallace (ed.), *The GDR in the 1980s* (Dundee: GDR Monitor Special Series no. 4, 1984).
[157] G. Wallraff, *Lowest of the Low* (London: Methuen, 1988). Depressing documentation of the experience of foreign workers in West Germany by a participant observer adopting the role of 'Ali'.
[158] H. Weber, *Die DDR 1945–1986* (Munich: Oldenbourg, 1988). Excellent narrative account and discussion of the literature and state of research.
[159] H. Weber, *DDR: Dokumente, 1945–1985* (Munich: dtv, 1986).
[160] H. Weber 'The Third Way: Bahro's place in the tradition of anti-Stalinist opposition' in U. Wolters (ed.), *Rudolf Bahro: Critical Responses* (New York: M. E. Sharpe, 1980).
[161] I. Wilharm, *Deutsche Geschichte 1962–1983*, 2 vols (Frankfurt: Fischer, 1985). Sequel to Steininger's collections.
[162] F. Willis, *The French in Germany* (Stanford: Stanford University Press, 1962).
[163] Wissenschaftliche Rat für soziologische Forschung in der DDR (ed.), *3. Kongress der Marxistisch-Leninistischen Soziologie: Lebensweise und Sozialstruktur* (Berlin: Dietz-Verlag, 1981). Some revealing contributions (on, for example, elites, and the perpetuation of social inequalities across generations), despite compulsory lip service to official East German platitudes.

[164] *Wörterbuch der Geschichte* (Berlin: Dietz, 1984). Official East German views of history.

[165] *Wörterbuch der Marxistisch-Leninistischen Soziologie* (Berlin: Dietz, 1977). Official East German views of Marxist-Leninist sociology.

*[166] R. Woods, *Opposition in the GDR under Honecker, 1971–85* (London: Macmillan, 1986).

Index